When Your Jewish Child Asks Why

Answers for Tough Questions

When Your Jewish Child Asks Why

Answers for Tough Questions

Kerry M. Olitzky
Steven M. Rosman
David P. Kasakove

KTAV Publishing House, Inc
Hoboken, New Jersey
1993

Library of Congress Cataloging-in-Publication Data

Olitzky, Kerry M.
  When your Jewish child asks why : answers for tough questions /
Kerry M. Olitzky, Steven M. Rosman, David P. Kasakove.
     p. cm.
  ISBN 0-88125-451-7
  ISBN 0-88125-452-5
  1. Judaism--Study and teaching (Primary) I. Rosman, Steven M.
II. Kasakove, David. P. III. Title.
BM105.043 1992
296.6'8'083—dc20   92-37176
                                                            CIP
Manufactured in the United States of America

TABLE OF CONTENTS

ACKNOWLEDGMENTS

As students and teachers of Torah, we are constantly in pursuit of knowledge. Through knowledge, we look for divine truth. In any endeavor there are many people to thank, too numerous to mention by name — even if we could remember all of those who have touched our lives and helped to shape us as we are today. Beyond the many contributors to this volume, we thank our students for asking questions and our teachers for helping us to struggle toward the answers. We also want to express our appreciation to Gordon Elliott, secretary of the School of Education at Hebrew Union College-Jewish Institute of Religion, New York, for his assistance in putting the pieces of this jigsaw puzzle together. Our publishers, Bernie and Sol Scharfstein, deserve more than praise; they are always unfailing in their support of our numerous projects.

Many at HUC-JIR, New York; at the Department of Religious Education of the Union of American Hebrew Congregations; and at the Jewish Family Congregation in South Salem, New York, deserve our thanks as well. In particular, we mention the names of Rabbi Norman Cohen and Kathy Thomson.

The support of our spouses, Sheryl Olitzky, Bari Ziegel, and Yael Kasakove, underscores each word that we wrote. And the discussions we had with our children, Avi and Jesse Olitzky, and Michal Rosman, are as much a part of our lives as it is of this book.

Our tradition teaches us that our children (*banim*) are our builders (*bonim*). This book is therefore dedicated to all Jewish children for they are truly the builders of our future.

Rabbi Kerry M. Olitzky
Rabbi Steven M. Rosman
David P. Kasakove

New York, New York
Rosh HaShanah, 5743

1

INTRODUCTION

Children love to ask questions. Sometimes their questions help them learn more about the world and its citizens: "Why can't there be peace all the time?" Sometimes their questions help them learn more about themselves: "Why do I sometimes do bad things?" Sometimes their questions help them learn more about living with other people: "Why do I get in fights with my brother and sister when I know I truly love them?"

The medieval Jewish sage Solomon ibn Gabirol taught that "the finest quality of the human being is asking questions." Anyone who spends any time around children knows that their penchant for asking "Why?" "How come?" "What is that?" and a hundred variants of these questions can be endearing some of the time and quite exasperating at other times.

Children's questions can make us feel wise or uneasy. Yet, *our* emotional reactions to our children's questions cannot be our primary concern. A child who asks us a question, any question, must receive a response that honors the very act of asking the question, helps him/her discover a response that addresses what he/she wants to know, and encourages him/her to continue asking questions. Some questions make this easy, while others do not. What happens when children ask us questions like: "Why don't Jewish people celebrate Christmas?" or "Why are there bad people in the world?" or "Where can I find God?" or "How can I truly be myself?"

We know that every adult cannot be an expert in all things. The first-century teacher Shimon ben Zoma believed that "the wise person is the one who can learn from everyone." There are times when all of us need to know where to turn for guidance when our own answers are not forthcoming. Perhaps this book will be a place to which you can turn when you need help.

The questions answered in this book are some of the most often asked questions we collected from Jewish children, ages five to nine, studying in synagogue schools all over the United States. These

3

children asked questions about God and Torah, about customs and rituals, about peoplehood and family life, and about the nature of life and themselves.

To help us formulate our own responses to our children's questions, we have gathered the advice of some of this country's most renowned experts in the fields of rabbinics, Bible, theology, child psychology, and education. These scholars span the entire spectrum of Jewish denominational life and modern child psychology. Since Judaism is not monolithic and has never spoken with one voice on any matter, and since there are many approaches to child development and education, we have included several responses to most questions.

Consult this book as you would a gentle, caring teacher. Consider the variety of advice you find in the introductions to each section and in the scholars' words, and blend it with your own wisdom and intuition. We would like to recommend that you not tell children your "answer," as if there were only one "correct" answer to the kinds of questions under discussion. Rather, we believe that it is most empowering and enriching to provide children with just enough guidance and information to help them discover their own responses. This way, we imagine a process whereby you and the teachers you have consulted become partners in the nurturance of a child's own sense of confidence, esteem for the child's own ability to discover meaning, and love of inquiry which is the basis of all wisdom.

CHAPTER I

Being Jewish

1. Why am I Jewish?

2. How do I know I'm Jewish?

3. What does it mean to be a Jew?

4. If you are not Jewish, can you become Jewish?

5. Why are there so many different kinds of Jews?

6. How can I truly be myself?

7. What will I be when I grow up?

Jewish children as young as four or five already ask questions like "Why am I Jewish?" or "How do we know we're Jewish?" Such questions show us that children at this age are beginning to perceive themselves as individuals, distinct from others in their world. They become aware, for instance, that some of their friends may not celebrate all of the same holidays they do or go to the same place to learn about God. This process of maturation, called individuation, is one of the most crucial aspects of our children's growth.

As our children grow older, they perceive more subtle differences between who they are and who others are. Whereas before they may have perceived broad distinctions between themselves and those of other faith groups, they may now recognize the distinctions between

Jews. Some Jews may attend different synagogues or observe different rituals or celebrate holidays differently. Now they might ask questions like "If you are Jewish, do you have to follow all the rules?" or "Why are there so many different kinds of Jews?"

These questions give us a chance to help our children form positive self-images, positive Jewish identities, and tolerance for others' differences. Indeed, some of the questions they ask may stump us. They may touch upon areas of our own beliefs which we still have not resolved, or make us uncomfortable. It is important to recognize that the nonverbal signals we send our children help to shape their growth as much as our actual verbal responses. Children recognize apologetic tones in our voices or discomfort in our faces. We best contribute to the positive Jewish identity formation of our children when we respond to their questions with love for them and pride for our heritage. And we contribute to their development of tolerance for others when our responses display a respect for all kinds of observances and for all kinds of people.

Why Am I Jewish?

A child has asked, "Why am I Jewish?" and you, the adult, need to respond. What to say? This is at once the simplest and the most perplexing of questions, for simultaneously it asks about a simple fact of genealogy, about a justification for living a certain kind of life, and about a mystery of meaning that none of us can truly fathom.

First and foremost, I am Jewish because it is my inheritance. Most children are Jewish through the agency of someone else. As a child, then, I receive the inheritance of Judaism as a gift and as an obligation from my parents.

Of course, this means that Judaism is usually something that I have received without much choice on my own part. And because of that, *inheriting* the tradition is only the first step toward really "being" Jewish. The classical rabbinic commentators make the same point when they distinguish between God's act of giving the Torah and Israel's choice to *receive* it. Receiving anything is not a passive matter; it is an active decision—whether that means, in a mundane sense, opening the letter that comes in the mail or adjusting the television for better reception or, in a deeper way, experiencing a work of art or a profound moment in nature. We open letters, but we open *ourselves* up to experiences. The person who has not opened him or herself up to Judaism cannot really receive what is being given.

Judaism, I said earlier, is a gift, but it is an obligation as well. Having been given Judaism without our choice, we could, of course, decide to reject it or ignore it. Living as free individuals in the modern world such possibilities of rejection exist; no one can convince another to be open to an opportunity that they want to decline. But before we reject what is being offered, we ought to consider first what's in the package. We have an obligation to give it a chance.

I would suggest three reasons why. First, because only a very foolish person throws away the container without first looking at the gift. Now, the worth and value of every gift is not always readily apparent. Judaism is a complex and multifaceted phenomenon. To understand it and appreciate it takes time and careful reflection. Because of that fact our tradition has placed the highest value on study: learn what is in the package and think hard about it. Like many difficult but rewarding things, deeper thought and richer experience tend to sharpen our appreciation for what Judaism is. The first time you listen to a certain kind of music you might not "get" it; the first time you see a sports event, you might not appreciate it. But as time passes and as one learns to listen or to watch, knowledge and appreciation grow as well.

Secondly, learning about Judaism is an obligation we have to where we have come from. Judaism is an ancient tradition, older by far than most of the things children know. Devoting time to learning about Judaism is something we owe to the past. There are things about Judaism that a person may come to reject, but before getting to that point, one needs to consider why this tradition has endured for so long and has been so important to those who came before us. I often say that Judaism is a lot like family. If someone tells me I am about to meet a family member I've never seen before, I feel a sense of obligation at least to give that person the benefit of the doubt before I say I don't like him! I think the same thing is true about Judaism.

Finally, Judaism is something beyond the lottery of who one's parents are and the genealogy of a rich past. Judaism is an opportunity to experience wisdom. The Jewish tradition offers a wealth of insight, depth and compassion that helps me grow, that helps me think about the biggest questions that human beings have ever asked: how are we meant to appreciate the world, how are we to treat our fellow human beings, what purpose is there in our existence. In an age that spends a great deal of time wrapped up in the trivial,

Judaism gives me the chance to ponder the deepest questions that people have ever asked.

Barry W. Holtz , Co-Director
Melton Research Center
The Jewish Theological Seminary of America
New York, New York

Why Am I Jewish?

Our Jewishness is one of the precious gifts our parents have given us, like food and clothing and home and hugs and protection.

Many of us are Jewish because one or both of our parents is Jewish. Through our birth into a Jewish home, or because our parents decided to initiate us into Judaism and the Jewish people by circumcision or a naming ceremony, we are Jewish. So our Jewishness is one of the precious gifts our parents have given us, like food and clothing and home and hugs and protection.

Our Jewish religion helps us feel God's presence, express our closeness to God in prayer, and discover how God wants us to live. We need our Jewish religion to help make certain times in our life special. We need our religion to help us face the difficult times when we are discouraged by failure or lose someone we love.

Being Jewish makes our little life part of a great story and gives our life a great purpose. We Jews learn we are part of a people who began with Abraham and Sarah. The Jewish people has been on earth for thousands of years because Jewish children, when they grew up and became parents, passed the Torah to their children, and because in every age some persons who were not born Jewish chose to become part of our people and our faith.

When we get older we begin to appreciate just how precious our religion is. Because we are a people small in number and have endured so much over the centuries, there is a special closeness to other Jews. We feel responsible for each other's safety and well-being whether in Israel or the countries that once comprised the Soviet Union, or Ethiopia. What we have endured has also taught us to be sensitive to the sufferings of all people.

Torah teaches us that we are Jewish not only because we were born Jewish or decided to join the Jewish people. We are Jewish because God has had a special covenant (relationship) with our people ever since the time of Abraham and Sarah. That covenant was renewed by Isaac and Rebecca, by Jacob and Rachel and Leah—and by all succeeding generations, including our own.

By being Jews we do something special for God in the world. We teach the world that only God is God. We Jews teach that there is something of God in each of us—but that no person, not even Moses, was more than a human being.

Torah teaches that when we observe Shabbat and try to love our neighbor as ourself, when we recite our Hebrew and English prayers, when we study how God wants us to live and do *mitzvot*, we are being the person God intends us to be, and we are helping to bring closer the day when God's reign of love and justice and peace will be established on earth.

Samuel Karff, Senior Rabbi
Congregation Beth Israel
Houston, Texas

Why Am I Jewish?

I *choose* to be Jewish because it is a lifestyle that places great importance on practicing good and right conduct toward others.

A good way for an adult to respond is by turning the question inward and answering it for oneself. For me, a simple answer to this question is to say, "I was born to a Jewish mother and father." That makes me Jewish by birth. But what makes me Jewish by any other standard? The answers are manifold. After having studied the Jewish religion and Jewish culture, and having lived among the Jewish people, I *choose* to be Jewish because it is a lifestyle that places great importance on practicing good and right conduct toward others. It is also a religion which, through its worship and system of belief, teaches the oneness of God and the unity of the human family. Judaism teaches that we are responsible for one another and that we must improve the world in which we live. For all of these reasons, I am proud to be Jewish.

Alfred Gottschalk, President
Hebrew Union College-
Jewish Institute of Religion
New York, Cincinnati, Los Angeles, Jerusalem

Why Am I Jewish?

Choosing to be Jewish means choosing to practice a religious faith that is free of fear. This is very different from a religion whose belief is based on a life after death and on statements of authority by a church.

Judaism's "separateness" is distinguished by a belief in doing rather than believing. When I understood that when Moses received the Ten Commandments on Mount Sinai, he received a set of guidelines that would help me live a productive life on earth—well, that was a big reason in my decision to embrace Judaism. This is why I am Jewish.

When I was preparing to accept the responsibilities that are essential to being a Jew, I was accepting a way of life whose main function would encourage me to attain higher levels of ethical behavior—to be the best person I could be.

Being Jewish has given me happiness, fulfillment, and an identity rich in history and meaning.

Being Jewish has given me happiness, fulfillment, and an identity rich in history and meaning.

Mary K. Bogot, Director of Volunteer Services
Mount Sinai Hospital
New York, New York

How do I know I'm Jewish?

There are two ways of becoming Jewish: the easy way and the hard way.

There are two ways of becoming Jewish: the easy way and the hard way.

The easy way is this: if your mother is Jewish, you are automatically Jewish—you are born that way.

The harder way is this: if you were not born Jewish, you can become Jewish.

If you were adopted, and your parents decided they wanted you to be Jewish, they could have you converted when you were very young.

Or, if you decided as an adult that you wanted to be Jewish, you could convert to Judaism.

Either way, once you have made the decision to convert, you are as totally and completely Jewish as if you were born that way.

You then spend the rest of your life discovering what it means to be Jewish, and making your life a Jewish life.

Deborah D. Miller, Director
Solomon Schechter School
East Brunswick, New Jersey

How do I know I'm Jewish?

From a strictly traditional point of view, you are Jewish if your mother is Jewish or if you complete a course of study and convert to the Jewish faith. From a Reform standpoint, you are Jewish if *either* of your parents is Jewish. So the simplest answer to this question is what we might call the argument from heredity. According to this argument, you remain Jewish from the time you are born or the time you convert to the end of your life.

Yet there are times when this answer is too narrow. For example, during the Holocaust the Nazis defined a Jew as anyone who had even one Jewish grandparent. In Nazi Germany, this became the official definition of a Jew. On the other hand, when a Catholic priest named Brother Daniel applied for Israeli citizenship under Israel's Law of Return which grants automatic citizenship to any Jew who wishes it, the Israeli courts ruled that he was ineligible, despite the fact that he was born Jewish. In this case, his present practice was considered more important than his heredity. Or, again, consider Albert Einstein, Karl Marx, and Sigmund Freud. Despite the fact that none of them actively practiced Judaism, they are all considered Jewish by Jews and non-Jews alike. Even Spinoza, who was excommunicated by his Jewish community, remains identified as a Jew. And Theodor Herzl, the father of modern Zionism, hardly practiced the Jewish religion, yet many Eastern European Jews placed his portrait on their walls and considered him the next best thing to a Jewish messiah because of the work he did on behalf of his people.

The question therefore calls for a better answer—one which accounts for the realities of everyday life. To the argument from heredity, we must add the argument from environment. What does this mean? Essentially, you are

You are Jewish if you are born Jewish or convert to Judaism, or if you consider yourself Jewish and Jews accept you, or if you practice Judaism and other Jews accept you, or even, in some cases, if non-Jews consider you Jewish.

15

Jewish if you are born Jewish or convert to Judaism, or if you consider yourself Jewish and Jews accept you, or if you practice Judaism and other Jews accept you, or even, in some cases, if non-Jews consider you Jewish.

Seymour Rossel
Author and Educator

What Does It Mean to Be a Jew?

The essence of Judaism is reflected in one's behavior. Does a person's acts reflect *Kiddush Ha-shem* (sanctification of God's name) or the opposite, *Hillul Ha-shem* (desecration of God's name)? The observance of *mitzvot* (commandments) is the foundation of Judaism. These *mitzvot* lead us to God, which is the highest Jewish value. Knowing how God wants us to act is the responsibility of every Jew. If we act in a way that is disgraceful, then God's name is desecrated and Judaism is discredited. It was Goethe, a German poet, who declared: "As a man is, so is his God." Thus, our actions speak louder than our words. God prefers that we fulfill the commandments. The rabbis state that God is supposed to have said to Moses: "It is more important that they do *mitzvot* than believe in Me." Therefore, the rabbis knew very well that performing *mitzvot* will lead to belief in God.

Since mitzvah is central to Judaism, we need to inquire as to what *mitzvot* we are talking about. What guidelines have to be followed? According to Jewish tradition there are 613 *mitzvot*, including some that are impossible to abide by today, such as offering animal sacrifices at the Temple in Jerusalem. How each of us will observe *mitzvot* is often based on which branch of Judaism we have chosen to identify with, and on the customs and priorities of our synagogue and community, whether positive—as in honoring parents or keeping the Shabbat, or observing the so-called negative commandments—thou shalt not steal or murder.

For me, the *mitzvot* that are to be practiced are those that enhance our lives and the lives of those around us, thereby bringing glory to God. These include observing the Shabbat and the Jewish holy days through prayer, study, and family togetherness; performing deeds of loving-kindness; the giving of tzedakah (charity); respecting parents; and showing concern for those less fortunate than we. The study of Torah is also central to being and acting Jewish. To discipline ourselves we should set aside a certain time for the study of a biblical chapter, or perhaps selections from the *Ethics of the Fathers* or a prayer from the prayerbook.

Of equal importance is to be part of the Jewish community. Hillel put it best when he said: "Separate not thyself from the community." To care for our fellow Jews is our responsibility.

This is what it means to be a Jew.

Bernard M. Zlotowitz, Senior Scholar
Union of American Hebrew Congregations
New York, New York

What Does It Mean to Be a Jew?

The question "What does it mean to be a Jew?" has called forth so many different responses in the past and present that no single answer is likely to suffice. My answer, though personal, is greatly influenced by traditional Jewish sources like the Tanakh and the Talmud.

For me, the meaning of being Jewish is summed up in the Hebrew word *mezuvveh*, "commanded." Being Jewish means *recognizing* that one is commanded. I believe that the One who commands is God. I find God's commands (*mitzvot*) in the Torah, which God revealed to Israel.

While this statement sums up my position, things are obviously—and in typically Jewish fashion—more complex. Why do I think commandedness is meaningful? For that matter, why do I think it important for God to be the commanding force in Jewish life? Further, how do commandments make being Jewish meaningful? These questions help shape my response to the opening question.

Being commanded means to stand in a relationship of responsibility to God, to my own people, to the world and its communities, and to myself as someone created in God's image. The tradition speaks of the "yoke of the commandments" (*'ol ha-mitzvot*); it is the weight of responsibility that constitutes this "yoke." Yet the realization that God believed that I and all of Israel could handle serious responsibility suggests that we are not merely subject to God. We are also capable, strong, and dignified parties somehow needed by God to help perfect God's creation. Thus, being Jewish means being God's helper, partner, and representative in making the world work.

I believe it is Jewishly important to recognize God as the One who commands because I believe that only God can know what is ultimately the right thing to do. While I believe

For me, the meaning of being Jewish is summed up in the Hebrew word *mezuvveh*, "commanded." Being Jewish means *recognizing* that one is commanded.

humanity is the crown of God's creation, I also know how the masterful and brilliant human mind can conceive of ethically horrifying and destructive ideas, justify them, and work out their execution. I do not believe the same to be true of God. Rather, I accede to the judgment of Moses, the person who knew God best: "God is the Creator whose work is perfect, all His ways are just; He is a trustworthy God, not unfair; He is righteous and moral" (Deuteronomy 32:4). God's commandments are, therefore a program for moral and life-fostering action in our world. Being a Jew means to "do the good and the moral in God's eyes" (Deuteronomy 6:18).

Accepting God in this way has not meant that Jews need not make any moral judgments. God's commandments tend to be general guidelines for action which leave us with the task of working out the details. The great works of the Jewish legal and ethical tradition—the Mishnah, Talmud, codes, responsa and *mussar* literature—all show how hundreds of Jewish generations in different times and places actively participated in *determining* how to observe God's commandments. Being commanded to act also means being commanded to think, question, study, and create the means for observing God's *mitzvot*. This, too, is how God has made us partners in the work of creation.

But how do *mitzvot*/commandments make being Jewish meaningful? First we need to recognize God's concerns, expressed in the form of relationships with fellow human beings, animals, and even things; concern for our spiritual development; the building of family, the Jewish people, and the world community. On one end of the spectrum God cares about things as "mundane" as physical hygiene (Deuteronomy 23:13-14), and on the other as "spiritual" as how we relate to Him/Her (Deuteronomy 6:5).

From my perspective, being Jewish is meaningful because living as a Jew means living all of life as a form of holy service. This gives me, and many other Jews who think as

I do, the fulfilling sense that all that we do is purposeful because it is directed toward helping God help us perfect our lives and our world.

In closing, I wish to add one short note. There are obviously Jews who do not believe in God or believe that God is the One who commands. Does my answer to the question "What does it mean to be a Jew?" exclude them from the Jewish people? My answer is a resounding no! While I have concentrated on what contemporary Jews would call the "religious" aspect of being Jewish, traditional Judaism did not separate Jewish life into "religious" and "secular" or "religious" and "ethnic." The Jews were—and are—a nationality with a highly "religious" culture and value system. This allows for "secular" identification with Jewish peoplehood, values, or culture as legitimate and meaningful ways of being Jewish. The breadth of *mitzvot* is so wide that there simply is no such thing as a self-identifying Jew not observing many of them. I took the question "What does it mean to be a Jew?" as a starting point for defining my sense of Jewish responsibility and the meaningfulness of Jewish living. I chose not to understand it as a request to define who deserves the cherished title "Jew." That is best left to the One who "chose Israel out of love" (Daily Prayers, morning service).

Michael Chernick, Professor of Rabbinic Literature
Hebrew Union College-Jewish Institute of Religion
New York, New York

If You Are Not Jewish, Can You Become Jewish?

In a word, the clearest answer to the question is "Definitely!" Consider this: The founders of the Jewish people, Abraham and Sarah, were *not born* Jewish—they *became* Jewish.

In a word, the clearest answer to the question is "Definitely!" Consider this: The founders of the Jewish people, Abraham and Sarah, were *not born* Jewish—they *became* Jewish when they were adults by virtue of the Covenant they entered into with God.

In time, the Jewish people consisted of more than Abraham and Sarah's family. The Torah states that when Abraham and Sarah left Haran for the Promised Land, a number of persons joined them (Genesis 12:5). Centuries later, when the Israelites embarked on their Exodus from Egypt, a large group of non-Israelites joined with them (Exodus 12:38).

Probably the best-known biblical character to become Jewish was a Moabite woman named Ruth. In these beautiful words she pledged her loyalty to the Jewish people and religion: "Your people shall be my people and your God my God" (Ruth 1:16). Both of these elements—the ethnic and the religious—are part of Jewish civilization, and, therefore, those who become Jewish enter both the folk and the faith of Israel.

The process of conversion (*gerut*) includes a lengthy period of preparation, including significant Jewish study, celebration of Shabbat and festivals, participation in Jewish community events, counseling sessions with a rabbi, and deep soul-searching. When the person feels ready to become Jewish officially, with the concurrence of the sponsoring rabbi, a conversion ceremony is held.

How does a person actually become Jewish? Circumcision (*milah*) for men and immersion (*tevilah*) in a ritual bath (*mikveh*) or a natural body of water for both men and women are required in the Orthodox, Conservative, and Reconstructionist movements and are optional in the Reform movement. All of the movements insist upon *kabbalat ol mitzvot,* the acceptance of the yoke of the command-ments. At the conversion ceremony, which traditionally takes place in the presence of a Bet Din (rabbinical court), the prospective Jew-by-Choice pledges to fulfill the com-mandments of Judaism and receives a Hebrew name. This ceremony can be private (with only the convert's nearest relatives and friends present) or public (at a Shabbat service, for instance).

In the open society in which we live, more and more people are exploring Judaism, many with the goal of ultimately converting. The household of Israel is greatly enriched by the addition of these new members of the community.

Stephen J. Einstein, Rabbi
Congregation B'nai Tzedek
Fountain Valley, California

If You Are Not Jewish, Can You Become Jewish?

Throughout history, Judaism has been enriched by people who chose it. Each year in North America, thousands of people who were not born into Judaism become Jews.

Throughout history, Judaism has been enriched by people who chose it. Each year in North America, thousands of people who were not born into Judaism become Jews. Led by a rabbi, they go through a period of studying and experiencing Judaism, which culminates in a moving ceremony during which they accept Judaism, cast their lot with that of the Jewish people and receive a Jewish name. From that moment, according to Jewish law, they are completely equal to Jews-by-Birth.

But at the beginning, legal reality is often very different from existential reality. The ceremony in which they accept Judaism signifies promise and potential. It marks their Jewish beginning—not their Jewish completion. Although they have studied diligently and are deeply committed to Judaism, they do not *yet* have a fully formed Jewish identity. They do not *yet* have a complete Jewish memory-bank, their own personal Jewish past. That will have to be formed as they have a Jewish life in the weeks, months, and years to come. The rabbis in the Talmud understood this very well. They taught that the new Jew-by-Choice will be formed in the same way that a baby's Jewish identity is formed—slowly and cumulatively as a result of years of learning and experience.

Along the way there will be many challenges. Developing a feeling of Jewish authenticity is often a major concern. In choosing Judaism, Jews-by-Choice are becoming part of a people as well as part of a religion. This ethnic or peoplehood dimension is often the most difficult to grasp. There is an enormous amount to learn in order to live a Jewish life, but there is also a *connectedness*—to the Jewish community and to Israel—that has to be developed.

24

Appropriately integrating one's non-Jewish past with one's Jewish present is another concern. New Jews-by-Choice must help their non-Jewish family understand that their choice of Judaism does not imply rejection of their non-Jewish family members.

These concerns can be resolved with time, patience, and experience. But one more element is required: sensitivity and receptivity on the part of the Jewish community. New Jews-by-Choice are frequently concerned about whether they will be accepted by the Jewish community. Our tradition requires us to know the heart of the stranger. This requires us to look deeply into our own hearts. Do we really believe that someone not born a Jew truly can become a Jew, can feel like us, can look out at the world through Jewish eyes? Understanding the difficulty of being a stranger in a strange land, can we provide an environment which will nurture the transition, the Jewish becoming, of those who have chosen to make our destiny their own?

As we reach out to those who choose Judaism, as we share our familiarity with Judaism, we come to see our own tradition through the eyes of one who is new to it. We value it anew and we come to understand that each of us, in order to live a life that is truly Jewish, must make Judaism an active choice.

Lydia Kukoff, Associate Director
Avi-Chai Foundation
New York, New York

If You Are Not Jewish, Can You Become Jewish?

To become Jewish if one is not born Jewish is known as conversion.

To become Jewish if one is not born Jewish is known as conversion. The Jewish people is open to those who would seek a place within our community. The more traditional forms of Judaism are not as open to conversion as is Liberal Judaism, but conversion is possible in the context of every part of Jewish life and those who convert to Judaism are given a special place in the Jewish community.

When one converts to Judaism, one becomes part of a religion. One who desires to become Jewish by choice is really saying that he or she wants to become a part of Judaism, the religion of the Jewish people. Once the conversion takes place, the convert becomes a part of the Jewish people and of Judaism, the religion of the people who call themselves Jews. Now this may seem very complicated, and sometimes it is, but the person who sincerely wants to be Jewish, and to participate fully in the religion of Judaism, will take the time to understand these distinctions.

Conversion to Judaism is a process that involves many things. First it involves the study of Judaism and the history of the Jewish people. Conversion, however, is not merely doing Jewish things, nor is it merely intellectual understanding that makes belonging to the Jewish people possible. Conversion requires, at the heart of it, an emotional commitment to the Jewish people in general, and to Judaism in particular. The one who converts should be fully aware of his/her emotional tie. Converts must be familiar with the rites and religious practices of Judaism and have the desire to fully participate in our rituals, including regular attendance at synagogue worship on Shabbat and holy days.

Once the intellectual, emotional, and spiritual components have been studied and confronted, the individual is ready to enter into Jewish life through a service of conversion. This service has differences, depending upon the branch of Judaism the individual is entering. For all Orthodox and Conservative and some Reform Jews, the act of conversion takes place at the mikvah, or ritual bath. Conversion for women consists of immersion; for men, of immersion and the drawing of a drop of blood from the foreskin to symbolize circumcision, or, in the case of those not circumcised, of circumcision. For many Reform Jews, a short service of welcoming the convert takes place in the synagogue before witnesses.

Steven E. Foster, Senior Rabbi
Congregation Emanuel
Denver, Colorado

If You Are Not Jewish, Can You Become Jewish?

Not only is it possible for someone to choose to become Jewish, but people have been doing it for centuries.

Throughout Jewish history, the rabbis have expressed strong feelings about those individuals who choose to become Jewish and to live a Jewish life. Though the attitudes of the rabbis vary, most comments are accepting and highly enthusiastic. The point is, not only is it possible for someone to choose to become Jewish, but people have been doing so for centuries. Many of these Jews-by-Choice have become role models who remind us how special it is to be Jewish.

How does someone become Jewish? Conversion, *gerut*, is a process which involves the study of Jewish theology, ethics, traditions, history, literature, and observance. It also involves experiencing Jewish holidays and life-cycle events. Little by little, Jews-by-Choice see how Judaism becomes a way of life. For some, this process takes years of study and practice. Others choose to formalize their commitment after learning the basics and then go on to learn more.

The conversion process culminates with a conversion ceremony. The Jew-by-Choice declares, either publicly or privately, in the company of family and friends, acceptance of the Jewish faith. This is done before three adult witnesses made up of no fewer than one rabbi and two knowledgeable lay people. This special group, or Bet Din, interviews the Jew-by-Choice about his/her decision to embrace Judaism. Some Jews-by-Choice also choose to fulfill the traditional halachic requirements of *berit milah* (circumcision) or *hatafat dam-berit* (a special ceremony for circumcised males who did not undergo ritual circumcision), and *tevilah*, ritual immersion in the *mikvah*.

Another aspect of the conversion ceremony includes a statement that the Jew-by-Choice has chosen Judaism freely and accepts Judaism to the exclusion of all other religious faiths and practices. S/he pleades loyalty to Judaism and the Jewish people under all circumstances. Accepting Judaism means promising to establish a Jewish home and to participate actively in the life of the synagogue and the Jewish community. Living a Jewish life involves a commitment to lifelong study of Torah.

It is important to understand that one who converts to Judaism is not converting into a new or different person. Though this person may be new to Judaism, his/her Jewish identity is informed by past experiences and relationships. Jews-by-Choice don't stop being who they are just because they choose to live as Jewish life.

While it is the responsibility of the Jew-by-Choice to study and practice Judaism, it is the responsibility of the Jewish community to welcome this New Jew warmly and enthusiastically into the Jewish community.

Nina J. Mizrahi, Assistant Director
Hillel Foundation
Washington University
St. Louis, Missouri

Why Are There So Many Different Kinds of Jews?

An ancient rabbi taught, "Any gathering that is for a holy purpose is destined to endure."

Jews have lived in many lands and have had many differing experiences, some happy, some sad. Out of these experiences Jews keep asking themselves, "What would be good or bad for the Jews?" The answers have been so numerous that it is remarkable that Jews can get together under one label. Indeed, the same label can cover a variety of opinions. Take, for example, Reform Judaism. Congregations that call themselves Reform worship in many different ways, some with heads covered, others that object to wearing a skullcap. When Reform was started 150 years ago, it tried to help Jews adjust to the ways of their non-Jewish neighbors. On the way it discarded so many traditions that many Reform Jews today are demanding more observance of age-old customs.

At the other extreme in Jewish life are the Hasidic Jews, who feel that the only way to preserve Jews and Judaism is to transfer ghetto traditions and customs to America, to wear clothes and hair styles that make them look different from everyone else, and to live in all-Jewish communities. We may argue as to which group is right or wrong. If we stop to think about it, we discover that the very variety and the arguments it produces are what keeps Jews and Judaism flourishing. As an ancient rabbi taught, "Any gathering that is for a holy purpose is destined to endure."

Malcolm H. Stern, Genealogist
American Jewish Archives
Cincinnati, Ohio

How Can I Truly Be Myself?

To be in touch with the solution is to answer one of the most compelling issues for people growing up in a world filled with extraordinary choices.

The world in which our young people live is flooded with messages about material products. The messages say that if you use or own a certain product, then you will attain a certain status. That status and role is supposed to satisfactorily answer the questions about the self. Yet, the answer offered by a product will last only until the next seasonal flood of new goods into the stores.

The definition of the self as a consumer always leads to a sense of being empty. Because it is superficial it always leaves a person feeling vulnerable. This vulnerability drives the person so afflicted into ever more intense activity to verify and validate his/her identity. Unfortunately this lifestyle brings only transient solutions. By defining the *I*, the very self, as an *it*, a thing, an individual's sense of self always feels alienated.

In order to develop a true sense of one's self a person must define who he/she is in *relationship* with other people. The only solid sense of self comes from doing. The more a person can do, the more a person is able to share life with others, with friends and family, the more authentic he/she will become. "To truly be myself" means being able to care about the needs of others and to be able to do something to help. It happens best when a person feels truly competent in meeting his or her own needs and the needs of others. The paradox is that we find our individuality best when we are in a sharing relationship with others.

The paradox is that we find our individuality best when we are in a sharing relationship with others.

William V. Lewit, Psychiatrist
Scarsdale, New York

31

How Can I Truly Be Myself?

If you really want to be true to yourself, you'll have to decide how you would like others to describe you and how you would like to describe yourself to others.

If you really want to be true to yourself, you'll have to decide how you would like others to describe you and how you would like to describe yourself to others.

Do you have enough information to solve problems?

Do you like to enjoy life?

Do you like to feel an important part of the world?

Do you like to feel special?

Do you like having enough power to make a difference in your own life and the lives of others?

If you answered yes to one or more of these questions, then being proud to be Jewish, learning about Judaism, and participating in Jewish life, both at home and in the synagogue, will help make your yes answers happen.

Being true to yourself as a Jew involves thinking about yourself as someone who celebrates Judaism and who advertises the values of special Jewish times in his/her daily life. For example, does the following description sound like you?

Just as the world grows older, I grow older. I can grow to act in more mature ways. Through social action, I can affect the maturity of the world, its environment and all humanity.

Would you be proud, if your friends introduced you to others with these words? A yes answer means that your life is like Rosh Hashanah, the Jewish New Year, because these words also describe this very important time on the Jewish calendar.

How do you like the profile below?

I am proud to be a Jew. I can and will assert my Jewishness. Judaism deserves my loyalty. I can be a light to others, guiding them on a path that leads to brave self-respect.

It is wonderful being Jewish and being true to yourself.

Howard I. Bogot, Director
Department for Religious Education
Union of American Hebrew Congregations
New York, New York

CHAPTER II

Wondering About God

1. Is there really a God?

2. How was God born?

3. Where can I find God?

4. How does God grade us?

5. Why do some people write G-d for the name of God?

6. Why does God make diseases?

7. Why do we pray?

According to the rabbis, when the Israelites encountered God at Sinai, each person heard the divine voice in a personal and individual way. Since there were 600,000 people at Sinai, we might take this to mean that God "spoke" to the assembled multitude in at least 600,000 different "voices," all at once. This is not a very difficult concept for children to accept, because many children are convinced that they have a very personal and unique relationship with God. For children, especially preadolescent children, God is a confidant, protector, surrogate parent, judge, rescuer, and constant companion.

If each person standing at Sinai apprehended God's "voice" in a unique way, it seems reasonable to suggest that when Jews, in turn, have spoken about God, we have done so in a variety of ways which reflect our own personal experiences, our verbal resources, the influence of our teachers and parents, our historical circumstances, and our orientation toward our Judaism. In order to make sense out of this variety of God-talk, it helps to be familiar with some of the major idioms of this language.

Classically, Jews have referred to God as omniscient (all-knowing), omnipotent (all-powerful), all-good, super-natural, and non-corporeal, or pure spirit. In this language, God is primarily the Creator of the universe, the Revealer of the Torah and all other instruction for life, the Redeemer of the righteous and meritorious, the Listener of prayers and Responder to them, and the Judge of all that is.

Existentially, God is the Other who can only be encountered in the most genuine and authentic relationship we might have. In this language, God is known as the "Eternal Thou," the One whom we can never objectify. Rather, God is always present and open to our encounter, everywhere and every moment.

For others, God is the "Power that makes for salvation." Rather than express God in human metaphors or supernatural terms, this language speaks of God as a process, a supreme combination of natural forces which grant humankind the potential to achieve self-realization, the moral grounding and power of the cosmos, and the creative energy or spiritual seed out of which the universe expanded and by which the universe is sustained.

If one were to survey all of Jewish tradition, we think one would discover that those who have spoken about God have done so in accordance with their world views, perhaps revealing more about how they believed the universe worked than about the nature of God. That is why Jews have spoken about God in so many different "languages," if they have spoken about God at all.

Children will speak about God and ask questions about God in ways which reveal a great deal about their world views and their own conceptual development. Sometimes their questions will be utterly concrete. Sometimes their questions will reflect current interests that they have, generally, about themselves and their world. In this case, they might be interested in the origins or births of things. In any event, they most certainly have a language all their own, and the most meaningful responses will attempt to reflect that language and respect that world-view.

Is There Really a God?

One of the strongest indications that a God exists can be found in the order of nature.

"God" means many different things to different people. Some of us imagine God as an all-powerful father who rewards us when we behave and punishes us when we misbehave. Others find God in the words of the Torah, or in the beauty of nature, or in the act of prayer. Still others believe that God is at work controlling events in history, maybe even moving the world close to a time when we will all live together in peace. All of these ideas about God are part of our Jewish tradition.

We cannot absolutely prove that any of these ideas about God is really true. Asking "Is there really a God?" is *not* like asking "Is the world really round?" or "Is two plus two really four?" even though it looks like the same sort of question. There is no completely convincing evidence to show that God really does or does not exist. Yet, if we pay close attention to the world around us, we may find indications that there is a God. But these are only clues or hints of God's presence in the world. Depending on their circumstances, most people at various times in their lives waver between believing and doubting that God is really there.

One of the strongest indications that a God exists can be found in the order of nature. Long ago, people observed the regularity of the seasons and the movements of the stars, and concluded that God was the source of this orderliness. Modern scientists have demonstrated that the universe is vaster, and life on this planet more complex, than we had ever imagined before. Also, the more we have learned to control our environment, the more we realize how much we do not control. There are powerful forces at work which keep the world turning and which make the seeds we plant grow into the food we need to live. The order and power of nature lead many people to believe that there really is a God, and that to survive we must respect the world as God has made it.

Many people also find God in their relationships with others. Human beings are biological creatures, but we are also much more than that. Unlike other animals, we can express a wide range of emotions, dream about the future, and empathize with the suffering of others. Above all, we can set goals for ourselves and strive to teach them, reflect on the meaning of our own lives, and develop deep relationships with others. As we do all of these things, we come to appreciate the spiritual aspects of life. There is within us the potential for evil and destructiveness, but there is also a source of great beauty and inspiration. The wonder and depth of human life itself leads many people to believe that God really does exist.

Both around us and within us there are powerful forces and deep mysteries. As we grow and change and become more attuned to the world, we may see glimpses now and then of God.

Louis E. Newman, Associate Professor of Religion
Carleton College
Northfield, Minnesota

Is There Really a God?

With no God, no architect who made the world with a plan and design and gave it a sense of meaning and purpose, then our lives would have no meaning, the world would have no redeeming value, and our lives would end in ultimate futility.

Philosophers over the years have wrestled with the difficulty of trying to prove or disprove God's existence. They have come up empty, unable to offer an irrefutable answer either way, so it would be ridiculous to add another, probably feeble attempt to this important question.

It is probably best to approach this question backwards. Let us for a moment assume a world without God. What type of world would it be? A world without God is a world without Godly values. A world without God is a world in which human beings are just ordinary animals except that they walk on two feet, with no Godly sanctity that emanates from their being God's creations. A Godless world is just a random reality with no purpose attached to it, since there was no architect that made the world possible. Existence is then an exercise in doing whatever you can to enjoy as much as possible, and in not caring about anyone else or anything else.

Such a world is a miserable world, with no caring, no lasting value, no focus on what is morally just and ethically upright. There is no law because there is no Judge; there is no value because there is no purpose.

It is perhaps in the consequences of a Godless world that we have the most potent argument for the existence of God. In simple terms, with no God, no architect who made the world with a plan and design and gave it a sense of meaning and purpose, then our lives would have no meaning, the world would have no redeeming value, and our lives would end in ultimate futility.

We have faith in God for the very same reason that we have faith that our life has meaning. The two go hand-in-hand.

Reuben P. Bulka, Rabbi
Congregation Machzikei Hadas
Ottawa, Canada

Is There Really a God?

Through sacred Jewish texts we come to know God in three ways—as the Creator, the Revealer, and the Redeemer.

Through sacred Jewish texts we come to know God in three ways—as the Creator, the Revealer, and the Redeemer.

I believe that the God of our ancestors really is the Creator of the universe because of what I have learned from science. Science uses mathematics to make intelligible all of the forces of change that occur in our physical world. The mathematical facts suggest that the universe has an origin. Whether it began by chance or on purpose goes beyond what any mathematician or scientist can determine. However, the overwhelming evidence of order in the universe makes it more reasonable for me to believe that it originated with purpose, by intent, rather than by chance. My belief that the universe exists on purpose supports my belief that there really is a God of creation.

I believe that the God of the Jewish people really is the Revealer for two reasons. First, when I pray I sense that there is an "other" with whom I communicate, and I know from reading that millions of other people also have this experience. Second, the Hebrew Bible has levels of meaning so deep that no matter how many times I read it, I learn something new. The genius of this work seems to me to so exceed any other work of literature that I cannot imagine its authorship to be entirely human. My belief that the Hebrew Bible is more than human supports my belief that there really is a God of revelation.

Finally, I believe that the God of Jewish texts really is the Redeemer of the world because of what I have learned from philosophy. Reality is more than what our senses report. There are also moral values that our minds discover. Beyond everything that is, we can discern what ought to be.

These "oughts" are standards that guide our behavior toward a single end, the redemption of the world. This end is the God of redemption. It is as real as the world's origin.

Finally, because I believe that God is One, I believe that the Creator, the Revealer, and the Redeemer are the same reality perceived in different ways. There is one God who really is the origin of the physical universe, who really is the "other" in communication, and who really is the end of morality. As Jews we know him as the God of our fathers—Abraham, Isaac, and Jacob, and of our mothers—Sarah, Rebekkah, Rachel, and Leah.

Norbert M. Samuelson, Professor of Religion
Temple University
Philadelphia, Pennsylvania

Is There Really a God?

I believe that all reality is divine. All of being contains sparks of mysterious cosmic life which we can see if we open our mind's eye to them. These sparks enable us to view all of existence as a single whole and give us a glimpse of life as being filled with absolute meaning. It is this vision—open to all who seek it—that I believe is the true vision of God.

The answer to this question depends completely on how you define two terms. What do you mean by "God" and what do you mean by "really"? Both of these must be open for examination.

I am a religious Jew. This means that I pray each day and that I open my heart to words of prayer that speak of and to Y-H-W-H (Adonai), the universal God of all being. This one God is described by our tradition as creator of the universe, as revealer of life's meaning, and as the one who will finally redeem the world. I affirm my relationship to *all* of these, but I understand *none* of them literally.

I do not know of any rigid lines that separate God, the world, and the human soul from one another. I believe that we discover Y-H-W-H when we turn most deeply inward, both toward ourselves and toward a more profound and "inward" perception of reality. Y-H-W-H should not really be translated as "God," which is a term that derives from old German paganism rather than from Judaism. The Hebrew term is really an impossible conflation of the verb "to be." Rather than "God," it should really be translated as "is-was-will be." Y-H-W-H means "God," but in a sense that is not separable from existence itself. The same letters, when rearranged as H-W-Y-H, means "existence" or "being." Y-H-W-H means: "That which is."

I believe that all reality is divine. All of being contains sparks of mysterious cosmic life which we can see if we open our mind's eye to them. These sparks enable us to view all of existence as a single whole and give us a glimpse of life as being filled with absolute meaning. It is this vision—open to all who seek it—that I believe is the true vision of God.

The figure of God imaged by most religion is a human projection. The person on the throne, to paraphrase one surprisingly radical Hasidic statement, is there because we put him there. No God-figure would exist had we not created or projected it. In this sense, my view can be called nonbelief. But we who create "God" are also created by Y-H-W-H. We are creatures of a natural world that itself is filled with divine mystery. I like to say that God creates us in the divine image and it is our task to return the favor. God seeks to make us divine. Conversely, we have a need to remake Y-H-W-H in the human image.

Here we must involve ourselves in a profound subtlety of religious language, in order to be quite clear. *All* the images through which we depict the divine, *both personal and nonpersonal*, are human creations. The reality toward which we are reaching through those images is entirely real. In religion, and especially in prayer, we are groping toward the essence of reality itself. But its nature is so subtle, the manner of its existence so profound, that *only* by means of projected images can we address it. We have to create such images, and at the same time we must ever be wary lest we turn them into idols.

I call the unitive essence of nature divine, not because of objective knowledge about it, but because all my attempts to encounter the world in its aspect of oneness evoke in me a feeling of an awesome presence—one that can only be described in the language of the sacred. As I stand "outside" my religious vocabulary, I know full well that "God" is a human projection. But as I seek a level of consciousness beyond that of my prosaic, "weekday" language, I know in the depths of my being that saying Adonai in prayer—itself an act of submission, substituting Adonai for Y-H-W-H, the mysterious and unutterable Hebrew name—is as close as I can come to naming and addressing the inexpressible mystery of life. This act of calling upon God, despite all I know about projection, is the essence of my religious faith. The human need to pray exists on an infinitely deeper level than the question: "Do you believe in God?" It is the desire to open myself to this level of reality that brings me back to faith.

Arthur Green, President
Reconstructionist Rabbinical College
Wyncote, Pennsylvania

How Was God Born?

The only honest answer to this, as to most questions about God, is that no one really knows. Any person who pretends to possess positive knowledge of God is, at best, suspect. The wisest men and women through the centuries have speculated about God, have tried their best to understand God, but none has entirely succeeded. You should respect the person who commences a statement about God with "I think" or "I believe" or "I am confident that." Be suspicious of anyone who says "I know" or "I am sure."

Human beings are born. Dogs, cats, flowers and plants are born—that is to say, we can point to a specific moment when their lives commenced. God is not a human being or a person. God surely is not an animal, a tree, or a bush. Therefore it really makes no sense to ask when or how God was born. We can tell approximately when different groups of people began to believe in God and their reasons for so believing. But that only reveals when human beings developed faith in God and why—not when God came into existence.

Religious people believe that God is eternal, that—unlike all other forms of reality—God had no beginning or birth because God has always existed. I know this must be difficult for you to understand. Although our understanding of God is necessarily limited, nevertheless, a variety of emotions and experiences have led us to conclude that a great Spiritual Essence, or Energy, or Thrust, is at the core of physical existence. In ourselves, as individuals, we call that Spiritual Essence "soul"; in the universe we call it God.

We do not ask when electricity was discovered or when the law of gravity began. These physical qualities or characteristics of the universe existed long before any human being developed enough intelligence or sensitivity to discover them. While comparisons of God to anyone or anything else are necessarily imperfect, we may say that in much the same way that electricity and gravity have always been characteristics of the universe, so God has been.

Roland B. Gittelsohn, Rabbi Emeritus
Temple Israel
Boston, Massachusetts

How Was God Born?

In responding to this question from a younger child, you would first need to make this simple statement: "God isn't like people. God didn't have to be born. God has always been here."

God isn't like people. God didn't have to be born. God has always been.

An analogy with other living things might help to illustrate this idea. Holding an egg, you could ask, "Where did this egg come from?"

"From a chicken," the child replies.

"And where did the chicken come from?"

"From another chicken."

Tracing the chain of life, you could explain that God was the Creator who started all the eggs and chickens, all the seeds and plants, or all the parents and babies.

An older child will likely be familiar with the above reasoning, but may want to know: "If everything in the universe has a beginning, how did God begin?" To respond, you might make reference to the mathematical notion of infinity.

"If a line is infinite in both directions, what does that mean?"

"It means that it has no end, either way," the child would respond.

"If the universe is said to be infinite in time, what does that mean?"

"It means that the universe has no end, that it will go on forever."

"But might it also mean that the universe had no beginning? Just as a line can be infinite in both directions in space, could a universe not be infinite in both directions in time? And if the universe is infinite, then so must God be, who formed the universe into order."

So far we have argued for a Creator-God who is coeternal with the universe; this may answer the question, but it leaves one rather cold. Therefore, I would suggest adding the following:

1. God has always been here because God is good and wants us to be good. Goodness may not always prevail, but it lasts forever because it comes from God.

2. God and we are growing together through time. Just as parents and children become closer as they both grow, so do we and God reach out for each other through time. We learn from God, and God learns from us. God continually gives us opportunities to improve ourselves and the world.

Lawrence A. Englander, Rabbi
Solel Congregation
Mississauga, Ontario

How Was God Born?

God wasn't ever born. God is the one, the only one, who never wasn't. God is the one, the only one, who was always here. God is the one, the only one, who made all the rest of creation, including you and me, possible.

God had no mother and no father. God was and is the mother and father of all that is created. God is the one, the only one, that was here before there was a before.

We don't fully understand how it was then, but we know enough about God to know that God never began to be, never had to. That is one reason we trust and love God and do not fear the future. Because, we believe, God will always be, just as God has always been.

Arnold Jacob Wolf, Rabbi
K.A.M. Isaiah Israel Congregation
Chicago, Illinois

God is the one, the only one, who never wasn't.

51

Where Can I Find God?

When I look up into the sky and watch the clouds slowly pass by in endless, glorious configurations, or gaze at butterflies fluttering in my yard, I think to myself, "These could not have been created by natural forces alone. They have been created by God and are a sign of God's existence."

Paradoxically, perhaps, though God is the creator of the world and all that dwells within it, actually *finding* God—as opposed to finding signs of God's existence—is not, I think, that easy. The problem as I see it is that you can't say "Now I'm going to find God" and automatically find God. Since God is invisible and doesn't call out to us in the same way that parents yell out the names of their children when they're looking for them, we have to be willing to invest some time in our search.

I am reminded of my son Abraham's photo album, which somehow got misplaced over a year ago. The photo album means a great deal to me, is something I want Abraham to have forever. It's a collection of the best photographs my husband and I took of him from the time he was born through his second birthday. Abraham loved looking through it and having me read the funny captions that I wrote underneath each picture, just as I loved looking at the album with him. The last time we saw it, I think, was in our basement—but I'm not sure. Every few weeks or so I say to myself, "Now I'm going to find Abraham's photo album," and spend anywhere from five minutes to an hour looking for it. I know the album's somewhere in our house and I am confident that I'll find it, someday, if I look in the right place. I guess that's why I keep looking for it—I know it's there and if I look hard enough I'll find it. There's always the possibility that I'll find it one day by accident. Frankly, I hope that happens. But I can't plan on that happening, so I keep looking and hoping it will turn up.

Finding God, I think, is not unlike finding my son's photo album—except that God doesn't just live in my house; God inhabits the entire world. On the surface, that seems to make the search for God even harder. If it's taken me a year to find a photo album in a house that has nine rooms (and I still haven't found it!), just think of how long it will take me to find God. But in fact the opposite is true. Although the world is much, much bigger than my house, God doesn't reside in just one place. In fact, God is everywhere all at once. It's as if the world were composed of millions of rooms and God was simultaneously in each of them. Moreover, unlike my son's photo album which is inanimate—that is, has no life or feeling—God *wants* to be discovered. Because our relationship is one of partnership, because *we need one another* to constantly recreate the world, both literally and figuratively, God reaches out to us, providing us with signs, or clues, that can help us.

When I look up into the sky and watch the clouds slowly pass by in endless, glorious configurations, or gaze at butterflies fluttering in my yard, I think to myself, "These could not have been created by natural forces alone. They have been created by God and are a sign of God's existence." When I witness even the smallest acts of kindness and compassion—when my five-year-old asks if I will help him write a get-well card to one of his friends who's been sick or when my three-year-old asks the mother of the boy whose birthday party he's attended whether he can have an extra balloon to bring home for his brother—I am struck by the fact that to be human means so much more than to simply physically inhabit the world. And again, I feel the existence of God.

The world is filled with such signs—with what my religious school teachers called "the hand of God." We can find such signs everywhere. And, remembering that we've seen such signs, we can search for God even when such signs aren't visibly present. Yet, like the search for my son's photo album, my search for God is often filled with frustration. "Where is God?" I sometimes ask myself, especially in times of great sorrow. But when I'm being truthful with myself, I admit that God *is* here, and that to find God I either need to look for more clues or, by opening myself to God, hope that God will find me.

Ellen M. Umansky, Associate Professor of Religion
Graduate Division of Religion
Emory University
Atlanta, Georgia

Where Can I Find God?

"Where shall I find Thee, and where shall I not find Thee?" asked Rabbi Levi Yitzchak of Berditchev, a hasidic master.

The Kotzker, another hasidic master, asked someone "Where is God?" and the person responded, "Everywhere!" "No," said the Kotzker. "God is where He is let in."

Shma Yisrael, Y-H-V-H is our God, YHVH is ONE!

Because we consider God's name, ׳ *yud.* ה *heh.* ו *vav.* ה *heh,* to be holy we do not pronounce it when we read it. Yet each one of the letters has special meaning. Still, it is better not to look for God as a noun or something that exists but as the infinite, never ending process of being and not existing.

Beginning with the last *heh,* we will explore the mysteries of the Name.

The aspect of God which we most often mean is that of the Creator whose work is perfect.

ה *Heh. It is perfect.*

God is the answer to the big *W*s: What, Who, Why, Where, When. God is a constant making, what made us be, whose designs we can only guess at, who must be underneath what is and makes it *be*! That One is not apparent to our sight. But at special times we can see how it fits together, how perfect it all is—even when we consider "flaws" or irregularities. How is it that everything that gets cold shrinks and gets heavy, yet water, when it freezes, expands? Figure what this world would be like if water in freezing shrank and sank to the bottom. There would be no life as we know it. So the perfection of the design points to a designer. This, then is God the Creator. The more science finds out about how

The Kotzker, a hasidic master, asked someone "Where is God?" and the person responded, "Everywhere!" "No," said the Kotzker. "God is where He is let in."

the universe began, the more closely it gets to what our religion teaches us and our souls' intuition teaches us.

Shma Yisrael, YHVH is our Creator, YHVH is ONE!

ו *Vav. You are loved.*

In our hearts we crave to hear one message—are we loved? Times occur when we know that there are no accidents in the world. God is a loving that is vaster than a parent's loving. This caring One who holds us in pleasure and in pain, who wills us to grow toward Her/His self. This is God, the great love.

That two bodies attract each other in space, the Law of Gravity is God, the loving, the flow in which people care for each other, the flow in which a cat licks her kittens clean, the flow in which, when you ask a question "Why?" there is another person caring enough to respond with an answer, "Because." Answering is a basic form of caring, and when the answering comes from God we call it revelation. And when we pray and we feel we are attended to—that loving is God. So too is the wanting to make babies, and the willingness to labor in giving birth, and the nursing that comes from close to the heart, that is the loving, and the arms that wait to receive one old and worn, one fatally injured and dying, that too is that divine loving.

Shma Yisrael YHVH cares for us. YHVH is ONE!

ה *Heh. All is clear.*

That we know anything at all is a wonder. That we know so much is overwhelming. That it all fits together is even more amazing. And that when we really know something well it also teases us to know more that we don't yet know it all. The clarity that makes sure, despite not knowing fully, that we know enough to do the right thing here and now, that also makes it clear that what we think is so—is really not so. That which is present to us in Torah and to other folks in the revelations addressed to them, that is God the Truth, the source of all knowledge.

God is an awareness that spans from knowing psions and muons, quarks that live nanoseconds and are gone, and at the same time being the awareness that contains a solar year, one in which the sun turns once around the galaxy takes 360,000,000 years. This awareness embraces all life and permeates each cell, each microbe and virus, beehives and anthills, rainforests and oceans. This awareness knows all not by "thinking" them but by being them—us and not being—at least 18,000 times each second. We are cells of Mother Earth's global brain, and her knowing is the knowing of God the *Melekh Ha'olam.*

Shema Yisrael, YHVH is Aware, YHVH is ONE!

Deeper in me than my own *I-am* awareness and your knowing your *I-am* awareness there is something vaster, more precious than existence, than love and knowledge. We call that "holy," sacred, a kind of God-special, enduring beyond what changes and enduring changes beyond our habits of enduring. That is sacred.

> That I-am-that-I-am is
> deeper than deep,
> higher than high,
> tinier than infinitesimal
> and bigger than infinite,
> older than ever
> and younger than now,
> beckoning and unapproachable,
> judging with utter truth
> and totally forgiving,
> longed for, adored and dreaded,
> avoided and ultimately embraced,
> with the deepest surprise
> "Hey, I am That!
> You are that,
> and this is That too!"

Shma Yisrael, YHVH is HOLY, YHVH is ONE!
So this is why we cannot say the word YHVH. We can't

do it with our mouth and mind, with our words and thoughts all at once.

It is perfect—the last *heh*, You are loved, the *vav*, All is clear, the upper *heh*, and I am holy, the *yud*.

Shema Yisrael
Yud Heh Vav He is
Our Creator,
who is aware of us,
cares for us,
is holy,
YHVH is ONE!
YHVH your God is Truth!

Zalman M. Schachter-Shalomi, Rabbi
P'nai Or Fellowship
Philadelphia, Pennsylvania

How Does God Grade Us?

Over a hundred years ago, a great rabbi who lived in the city of Baghdad was asked the following question: "A person has two kinds of bread for Shabbat. One is savory and tasty, but its appearance is somewhat unattractive, the crust a little dark; the other looks exquisitely white, but it has a sour taste. Which bread should be placed on the Shabbat table, the one that looks bad but tastes good, or the one that looks good but tastes bad?"

The rabbi, whose name was Rabbi Yosef Chaim, responded by stating that the good-tasting bread, even though it does not look quite as pleasing, is preferred. The spirit of this question and answer sheds light on the question: how does God grade us?

God does not grade us based on the way things look on the outside, but rather the way they truly are, through and through. A similar idea is expressed in the talmudic definition of who is rich? The Talmud says, "Who is rich? The person who is satisfied with what he or she has." Here again, the real definition of rich is not how things look from the outside, but rather how things really are—on the inside. A person is not rich based on how much money is in the bank; we all know people who have more money than we do but who are hardly richer in the deepest sense.

So it is with all of life. We must assume that God is not fooled by superficial appearances. We must assume that God does not grade us by how things look. Instead, we believe that God sees all and knows all, and takes everything into consideration. For example, we believe that God takes effort into consideration: the person who does not appear to be as good as someone else might actually be trying harder than the one who appears to be the better person. On the

God does not grade us based on the way things look on the outside, but rather the way they truly are, through and through.

outside we cannot see who is making more of an effort, but God sees the inside and judges accordingly.

How does God grade us? Perhaps He grades us as an ideal parent grades a child: with compassion, with understanding, with love. Not with harshness, not with a quick temper, not in a superficial way. Like the bread that does not always look good on the outside but is tasty on the inside, we believe that God sees beyond the surface and grades us accordingly.

Arthur Kurzweil, Vice President
Jason Aronson, Inc.
Northvale, New Jersey

How Does God Grade Us?

If life were a school and we were the pupils and God were the teacher, grading would be in order. What would we be expected to learn? First we would be expected to learn about our heritage—our holidays, customs, and traditions. Thus we would know that Judaism is to be practiced and celebrated year-round, at all times, not just once in a while or sometimes. To learn this in our early years is very good. Some people don't learn this until later in life. That's not as good, but later is better than never.

As we get older, we are to learn Jewish values. We call this learning Torah. Torah is what we must not do and what we most certainly are supposed to do. Learning Torah means that we must know right from wrong; we must know what is worthwhile and important, and what is foolish and not worthy of us. When we learn Torah, then our grades would be very high indeed.

What does learning about holidays, customs, and traditions have to do with learning Torah? Well, every time we do a Jewish act—light Shabbat candles, say a blessing, celebrate a holiday—we remind ourselves that we are Jewish and that we are a Torah people. That, in turn, reminds us that Torah people—

Do what is right
   (we don't steal or lie or become untrustworthy, we keep the commandments);
Care about others
   (we visit the sick, feed the hungry, rescue the captive, honor our parents);
Work to make this a better place to live
   (we keep the environment clean, lend a helping hand,

If God grades us, then it is according to how we use our Torah learning and the values of Judaism in making this world a better place for everyone.

do *tzedakah*, acts of righteousness and charity, and *gemilut chasidim*, acts of loving-kindness);
Preserve life
(we take good care of ourselves and those we love, look for ways to encourage peace at home and in the community, act like a *mensch*).

If God grades us, then it is according to how we use our Torah learning and the values of Judaism in making this world a better place for everyone. Some score high in knowledge, but only average in how they act. Some don't know much, but score high in what they do —in mitzvah work. The best grades would go to those who *learn* Torah and then *do* Torah—who learn what it means to be a Jew and then act as best they should.

But, in reality, this world isn't a classroom and you aren't the pupil and God isn't the teacher. Instead, the world is really in you, and you are both the pupil and the teacher— the learner and the doer. So, it's in your hands to do the grading on what you learn and on how you act. Nu? How are your grades so far?

Raymond A. Zwerin, Rabbi
Temple Sinai
Denver, Colorado

How Does God Grade Us?

God grades us according to our deeds, which should be modeled after the Thirteen Attributes of God, specified in the Bible.

When, after being given the Ten Commandments, Moses asks God, "Show me Your ways, that I may know You and continue in Your favor" (Exodus 33:13), the Lord proclaims: "The Lord, the Lord, God is compassionate and gracious, slow to anger, abounding in kindness and faithfulness, extending kindness to the thousandth generation, forgiving iniquity, transgression and sin; yet He does not remit all punishment" (Exodus 34:6-7).

Therefore, all human beings must strive to be "Godlike"—that is, compassionate, gracious, slow to anger, kind, faithful, forgiving, yet not absolving all guilt (like that resulting from premeditated murder; for example, the Holocaust). By thus imitating God's behavior, we glorify Him here on earth and please Him, while enhancing our own inner selves and making the world a better place for all people.

Note that these divine characteristics are very "democratic" in that they can be attained by everyone, regardless of age, station in life, class, wealth, rank, intelligence, looks, physique, religion.

The Talmud tells of a town being asked to declare who is its very best Jew. "The rabbi," say the townspeople in unison.

Comes the surprising response: "Certainly, the rabbi is a very good Jew, but he is not this town's *best* Jew."

"The philanthropist, then," say the people.

The response: "A very good Jew, but he is not the best Jew either."

> **God grades us according to our deeds, which should be modeled after the Thirteen Attributes of God, specified in the Bible.**

Other worthy candidates are named, but they too are rejected. "Who, then, is the town's very best Jew?"

The Talmud's reply: "See those two poor clowns? They devote their working lives to making people smile. And when they see someone sad, unhappy, in despair, they go out of their way to cheer him or her. So this town's very best Jews are those two clowns."

Then there's the Yiddish tale about a stranger who comes to town to look up a man whose name he's forgotten. The stranger describes the person as elderly and overweight, blind in one eye, with a facial tic and a hump on his back, dragging a lame leg.

"Oh," reply the townspeople, "You must mean Shloime. *A sheine Yid*. He's a *beautiful* Jew."

So you see, anyone at all can be "beautiful" or "the best"—Grade A in God's sight. Provided he or she treats others with loving-kindness. All it takes is a caring heart, the will, and—above all—the deeds.

Herbert Tarr
author of The Conversion of Chaplain Cohen
and Heaven Help Us

How Does God Grade Us?

In our daily life, we are often evaluated by others, such as parents and teachers. Yet few individuals, among them our parents and really good friends, know all aspects of our lives. Most people see only that side of us which they encounter in our meetings with them. Yet they form judgments about us, often unfairly, on the basis of that limited exposure.

On the other hand, it is not uncommon for us to assess our own achievements. We may not know how we sound until we hear ourselves on a tape, or know what we look like unless we look into the mirror, but in our heart of hearts, we do realize whether we are capable of accomplishing more, or whether we are consciously falling behind our abilities.

From experience, we are also aware that the way we see ourselves often determines the way others see us. In the Bible, when the spies returned from the Holy Land, they told Moses that they had seen giants before whom they appeared as "grasshoppers" (Numbers 13). We can learn from this text an important lesson: If you see yourself as a "grasshopper," ready to be crushed by others, you will soon act like one, and will end up being a prey to others. But if you see yourself as created, as the Bible says, "in the image of God" (Genesis 1), representing the highest values in our tradition, such as being charitable, loyal, peace-loving, then you will be moved to act in this high manner.

Once in a while, knowing that others judge our actions, we wonder how would God grade us. In reality, we do not know the answer to this question, for it often depends on what we mean by "God." And there are many definitions of it in Judaism. But underlying them all, there is an assumption that "God" represents important ethical values that we all cherish. We are urged, over and over again, "to walk in

The more we reflect the principles that God represents, the higher will be the grades in our own eyes, in the eyes of those who behold us, and hopefully, in the "eyes" of God, who represents in our educated conscience the best of all human and ethical values.

the path of God," that is to say, to appropriate those values which God represents and carry them out in our daily life. Then we will end up having a higher image of ourselves which is deserving of approval, praise, and emulation.

This does not mean, however, that we are expected to be perfect. No human being is ever perfect. All we need is to do our best. For our finest efforts, even if they fall short of the ideal, are always welcomed, as long as we are determined to do better tomorrow. Consequently, the more we reflect the principles that God represents, the higher will be the grades in our own eyes, in the eyes of those who behold us, and hopefully, in the "eyes" of God, who represents in our educated conscience the best of all human and ethical values.

Rifat Sonsino, Rabbi
Temple Beth Shalom
Needham, Massachusets

Why Do Some People Write G-d for the Name of God?

What is important to any culture is often called by many different words or descriptions. For example, Eskimos have a variety of names for "snow." People who live in the desert have many different words for "camel." And it is not surprising that the Jewish people have many different names for God, each revealing a different aspect of His essence.

Jewish tradition relates that the name of God—consisting of the four Hebrew letters ה ו ה י *yod, heh, vav, heh*— was revealed to Moses at the burning bush. Its exact pronunciation was passed on to his brother Aaron and kept a secret among the priests, so that the Israelites would not use God's name irreverently. The only time when the high priest actually pronounced the real name of God was on the Day of Atonement, during the confession of sins. When he uttered the holy name, his voice was lost in the singing of the other priests so that the Israelites would not hear the secretive pronunciation.

Outside of the ancient sanctuary the term Adonai was used to connote God's name. Whenever the original four Hebrew letters are found in the Bible, or when God's name is invoked in prayer, it is pronounced Adonai. But even this name of God is confined to use during sacred events. In conversation, the name HaShem, meaning "The Name," is often used to protect God's name ever further from possible blasphemy and improper use.

Jewish law has always tried to protect the way in which people use the name of God, always fearing the possibility of God's name falling into a bad mouth. The rabbinic sages prescribed a variety of injunctions concerning both the pronunciation and the writing of God's name. For example, if written, the name of God cannot be erased and can only be discarded through ritual burial, similar to that of sacred texts and ritual items.

The restrictions against writing God's name, although usually applicable only to Hebrew names, have been extended by various traditionalists to include the writing of the name in the vernacular. Thus, a meticulous Jew today might write the name of God as "G-d." In this way one would protect himself against the possibility of writing His true name in vain.

Ron Isaacs, Rabbi
Temple Sholom
Bridgewater, New Jersey

Why Does God Make Diseases?

Quite simply, we just don't know the answer to this question. We do know that some diseases are the result of the breakdown of the cells due to the aging process. Just as parts wear out in a car, a light burns out, a fan belt breaks through use, so too the aging process causes gradual deterioration of our bodies. With a car, however, many parts can be replaced. With the human body, we are just learning how to replace parts—through transplant operations. But these operations are costly and have high risk factors. It is also difficult to obtain organ donors and tissue matches.

Other diseases are the result of abuse of our bodies. Increasingly, the scientific and medical communities teach us that if we smoke cigarettes we are more susceptible to diseases of the pulmonary system, such as cancer and emphysema. If we eat the wrong type of food, too many fats, we clog our arteries and are more susceptible to cardiac problems: heart attacks, arteriosclerosis, high blood pressure. The abuse of drugs and alcohol has a poisonous effect on our organs, brains, and immune systems. Thus sometimes there are ways to help prevent diseases.

God as Creator, who made us all, gave us our bodies. But God also gave us the responsibility to care for our bodies by getting the right nourishment, proper exercise, and sleep. Showing the right respect for ourselves and our own bodies is one way we practice *kedusha*—holiness. We can model holiness in our everyday life through a daily regime of healthy living. These choices include a balanced diet. It includes keeping tabs on our health by seeking regular medical check-ups. Healthy living also means paying attention to our emotional lives. Increasingly, we are discovering the effect of too much emotional stress on our physical

God as Creator, who made us all, gave us our bodies. But God also gave us the responsibility to care for our bodies by getting the right nourishment, proper exercise, and sleep.

selves. In these ways we can practice God's *mitzvot*—God's commandments; to save and protect life.

Still, there are some viruses and diseases that we know very little about. For example, the common cold is a virus. Yet we still have no cure for it. We do not understand its purpose or why God created this virus. One explanation that circulates is that all things are part of the ecosystem of life—from the smallest parasite (some viruses are similar to parasites) to the largest mammal, the whale. But this explanation leaves us wondering about the benefit of some diseases, like the bubonic plague or cancer or AIDS. The devastating effects of these diseases on human beings leave us with many more questions than answers.

We also must be aware that these ideas are of little comfort for those who have these diseases and for their families. Therefore, we must learn to look at this question from a different angle. We must learn to look at the *way* we live and the *quality* of life we are able to have and provide for others. The Book of Psalms says, "Teach us to number our days, so that we may get us a heart of wisdom" (Psalm 90). Instead of believing we live forever, knowing our time is finite causes us to look at how we live each day, how we lead holy lives.

Devastating diseases without cures often cause those afflicted (both the patient and family and friends) to look at life very differently; not as a right, but as God's gift to us. If we all lived our lives as a precious and special gift from the source of being, no doubt we would view our days differently.

The many researchers who are searching for cures have increased our knowledge about the incredibly complex and wonderful human body. But as much as we know about how the human body works, there is still much we have yet to understand.

Certainly, our God as Creator inspires us with awe when we consider the complexity and wonder of the human body.

We should celebrate the grandeur of life, and our ability to participate in it, when we look at the miracle of the human body.

Denise L. Eger, Rabbi
Congregation Kol Am
Los Angeles, California

Why Do We Pray?

In the Torah, we are commanded "to serve Adonai, your God, with all your heart and with all your soul" (Deuteronomy 11:13). The rabbis interpreted "the service of our hearts" to refer to the act of prayer. From one perspective, then, we can answer this question by explaining that God commands us to pray, and this is why we do so. Through the act of prayer, we identify ourselves as members of a sacred, covenantal community. When we say the Shema together in unison— "Hear, O Israel, Adonai is our God, Adonai is One"—we affirm our link to Jews throughout history, as well as our link to our fellow Jews around the world.

Sometimes, though, a child may not be satisfied with such a "large" answer. The child may really want to know why she, as an individual, is being asked to pray. He may be confused about whether God actually listens to his prayers. She may wonder if God will answer her petitions. When answering such difficult questions, I recommend that we focus on the *act* of prayer itself, and discover with the child what it is that makes prayer a valuable experience. According to Jewish tradition, the precedent for the three daily prayer services began with the patriarchs: Abraham, Isaac, and Jacob. By exploring possible reasons why they prayed, we can find reasons why we pray.

It is said that Abraham instituted the morning (*shacharit*) service: "Next morning, Abraham hurried to the place where he had stood before God" (Genesis 19:27). Abraham is known as the founder of Judaism, the first one in the history of humankind to declare God's sovereignty. In a world of idolatry, Abraham dedicated his life to praising the Eternal One. Like Abraham, when we pray, we praise and give thanks to God for life's many blessings. In our busy lives, we all tend to overlook the many blessings that life has to offer—the blessings of love, of health, of knowledge, of nature. Prayer slows us down so that we can "count our blessings" and appreciate the world anew.

It is said that Isaac instituted the afternoon (*mincha*) service: "And Isaac went out meditating in the field toward evening" (Genesis 24:63). It is ironic that although the name Isaac derives from the Hebrew word "to laugh," Isaac was a very introspective, meditative person. From Isaac's example we learn that the act of being self-reflective, of meditating on one's life, is another reason why we pray. We have a tendency to be too quick to mask life's difficulties with a laugh. Prayer gives us the time to consider our place in the world, to wrestle with the mysteries of life. Prayer teaches us to be unafraid to face our deepest fears and concerns. This is another reason why we pray.

It is said that Jacob instituted the evening (*ma'ariv*) service: "Jacob . . . came upon a certain place and stopped there for the night" (Genesis 28:11). This phrase has been interpreted to mean that Jacob "encountered God." Of the three patriarchs, Jacob was the most demanding of God. He was never shy to ask for God's protection. In the same chapter of Genesis, Jacob asked God specifically for "bread to eat and clothing to wear" (Genesis 28:20). This, too, is an important reason to pray. Prayer gives us the opportunity to articulate our needs and our wishes. Often, we may find it difficult to express what it is we really want out of life. The process of petitioning God helps us learn about our identity. Though we may not be able to say with certainty whether God answers our prayers directly, nonetheless, the act of asking, in itself, helps us grow and learn about ourselves and our priorities.

It is through discovering these three elements—praise/thanksgiving, self-reflection, and petition—that prayer can become meaningful for the child. Through these three aspects of prayer, the child is enabled to refine and strengthen her character and, in so doing, connect with prayers and hopes of the Jewish community, from the time of Abraham to our own day.

David P. Kasakove, Director
Department of Media and Communications
Department for Religious Education
Union of American Hebrew Congregations
New York, New York

CHAPTER III

Talking About Torah

1. Did God really say what was in the Torah?

2. Are we supposed to believe everything in the Torah?

3. Which Bible stories really happened?

4. Were Adam and Eve really the first people?

5. Why did Abraham decide to be Jewish?

6. Did God really part the Red Sea?

7. Does God talk to me like God spoke to Moses?

As children, many of us read Bible stories or heard them read to us. Actually, the research of Bettelheim, Piaget, Paley, and others would seem to recommend that children in the primary grades ought to read Bible stories as one of several kinds of introductions to Torah. According to their studies, the world of story, especially fairy tales, accurately reflects the way children view reality. Four-, five-, six-, seven-, and eight-year-olds believe inherently in magic, in miracles, in animism, in kings and queens, spirits and demons. Since the Torah also speaks of kings (God), miracles, and wondrous deeds, children generally have no trouble accepting aspects of the biblical text which many adults would characterize as fantastic. Most often, the questions raised by children are not the products of disbelief or incredulity. They are, instead, as matter of fact as any other questions the same childen might ask about the events of any other stories they have read or seen on TV. Indeed, we adults often project our own difficulties relating to the more "wondrous" parts of the biblical text onto the psyches of our children.

Eventually, our children mature and begin to see the world according to a different set of constructs. Now they ask us questions about Torah narratives and other literary selections which would not have occurred to them even a year or two earlier and which now have a basis in disbelief or incredulity. "Were Adam and Eve really the first people?" "Did God really say what is in the Torah?" "Did God really part the Red Sea?"

To these questions, we have developed two primary catagories of response over the years. On the one hand, the classical rabbinic response to these questions is based on the premise that every word of the Torah was revealed to Moses on Mount Sinai and transmitted without error through the generations until the text was written down in the form and content which still exists today. When one responds from this perspective, God really did say what is in the Torah, Adam and Eve really were the first people, and God performed all kinds of miracles, including the parting of the Red Sea.

On the other hand, beginning in the nineteenth century, some Jews and Christians began to view the Torah text as the result of a human redaction of oral teachings and traditions which evolved over perhaps as many as eight hundred years. As Rabbi Gunther Plaut writes in his response (see below, p. 78), while many agreed "that Torah was the result of literary and religious evolution, we have continued to insist that God did play a role in this development, but not in the way tradition had depicted it. This makes Torah a book conjointly authored by God and by our people." If Torah is a product of human efforts and understanding, then one need not accept every verse and phrase literally. Rather, each reader is free to read the text with the same interpretative tools applicable to other kinds of literature.

Yet Torah is not simply any kind of literature. While novels, epics, legends, and tragedies seek to convey something about human existence, human nature, enduring values and ideals, Torah teaches about God (however, you wish to understand this appellation), the very source of those enduring values and ideals; the relationship of humankind and God, the relationship of a particular people, the Jews, and God, and humankind's attempts to apprehend God's messages for us, which are to be found everywhere we turn.

Did God Really Say What Is in the Torah?

While it may be agreed that Torah is the result of literary and religious evolution, God did play a role in this development, but not in the way tradition had depicted it. This makes Torah a book conjointly authored by God and by our people.

Whenever we speak of who God "really" is or what God "really" does or says, we are in the realm of mystery and uncertainty. So, to answer your question, let us start with tradition . . .

The idea that every word in the Torah is of divine origin was shared for thousands of years by our people and continues to be shared by Jewish and Christian orthodoxy.

But over time, this concept raised difficulties. First of all, there are obvious and numerous contradictions in the Torah. Secondly, it became increasingly difficult to explain how a merciful and compassionate God could approve of slavery, order the wholesale extermination of conquered nations, make the breaking of Shabbat rules a capital offense, or be interested in the minutiae of incense burning and other aspects of the sacrificial cult.

Slowly, therefore, the idea gained ground that the Torah came into existence not in the way we had always believed but in some other fashion. Beginning in the middle of the nineteenth century, Christian scholars and progressive rabbis began to view the creation of Torah not as a one-time event that happened at Sinai, but as a long process of development which may have taken as long as eight hundred years. By and large, Liberal Jews have accepted this idea, but—and here is the most important point to remember—*while it may be agreed that Torah is the result of literary and religious evolution, God did play a role in this development, but not in the way tradition had depicted it.* This makes Torah a book conjointly authored by God and by our people. How is this possible?

We start with our people. They developed the concepts found in the Torah over a period of many generations. In that sense, Torah is a human document. But it is more. This tradition was handed down by pious men and women who saw themselves as servants of the Almighty—and it is my belief that in a mysterious way, God was indeed at their side, guiding their work. To me, Torah is the attempt to reach God. In this way, Torah arose from the meeting of God and God's people. Not every word in the Torah may be a witness to this meeting, but every word was meant to try and come closer to God.

There is therefore no contradiction between treating the book as a literary document on the one hand and as a religious testimony on the other. The most important thing is to approach Torah with respect, because we do not really know when God speaks. But when we study Torah we may hope that through its words the divine voice will address us.

W. Gunther Plaut, Senior Scholar
Holy Blossom Temple
Toronto, Ontario

Did God Really Say What Is in the Torah?

Torah is like an echo of a voice. The voice we call the voice of God was heard by Adam and Eve, by Sarah and Abraham, by Moses, by Miriam at the Red Sea, by Jeremiah and Rabbi Akiva. It is often especially difficult for modern people to understand this echo.

God speaks to us in the Torah through the interpretations of teachers and through the creativity of our own minds when reading Torah. The Torah is a sacred book because it contains the words of human beings who sensed or believed that God was speaking to them—and through them to others. We read for example, "And God said, 'Let there be light,' and there was light." Despite everything we know scientifically about sunrises and sunsets, it is still a wonder how light banishes darkness. These changes in nature reveal a power in the universe beyond anything we can comprehend. That power is called God.

The Torah is a record of our search for what God wishes us to know—about our world, about ourselves, about the power that helps us see order and purpose in life. Rabbis, poets, artists, philosophers, students, and mystics have tried to explain, in different ways, what God said in the Torah. Through them we have many ways of knowing what Torah teaches us in our own day. What we learn from our teachers in each generation is part of what God has said in the Torah.

Recall the story of Jacob fleeing from Esau. Jacob puts his head to rest on a rock and dreams that angels are going up and down on a ladder, with God standing on top, saying, "I am with you and will keep you wherever you go and bring you back to the land" (Genesis 28:15). Here Jacob has had an experience that could happen to anyone running away in great fear. But still he feels protected; he is not alone. Whatever our fears, we have a drive to go forward, a faith in our hopes and dreams. I believe that this faith is the spirit of our ancestors. It is God's voice speaking through the Torah, and all that it has inspired over the centuries.

Torah is like an echo of a voice. The voice we call the voice of God was heard by Adam and Eve, by Sarah and Abraham, by Moses, by Miriam at the Red Sea, by Jeremiah and Rabbi Akiva. It is often especially difficult for modern people to understand this echo. For example, the voice tells what a small, weak people needed to do in order to survive in the midst of hostile, warlike peoples, in a world ruled by force. Now that we are dwelling in our own land God reminds us never to forget what it was like to be slaves in Egypt. I believe this is the echo we may all hear if we are to be deserving of the blessings that come to us; our homes, families, work, our land. The repeated mention of Egypt in the Torah and in our prayers is part of what God whispered to Moses at Mount Sinai, and which Elijah heard as a "still small voice" from within.

It doesn't bother me to describe God's ways as I describe the ways of a person. I realize this is only metaphor. Though we can never know anything absolute about God, we can use our imagination and employ our faculties of reason and conscience. Rabbi Ishmael taught, "The Torah is written in the language of human beings." This was the only way that an almighty God could make the Torah comprehensible to creatures of flesh and blood.

Shaul R. Feinberg, Associate Dean
Hebrew Union College-Jewish Institute of Religion
Jerusalem, Israel

Are We Supposed to Believe Everything in the Torah?

Whether we should believe everything in the Torah depends upon what we mean by "Torah."

In its most inclusive sense, "Torah" refers to the totality of Jewish religious tradition. In my view, Jews are obliged to accept that tradition as the basis of their self-understanding as Jews. But, while one is obliged to accept all that has been bequeathed as one's heritage, one is not obliged to believe in everything that has been accumulated by tradition. Indeed, since the Torah, the tradition, is so vast, and since it contains such a wealth of ideas—some in logical conflict with others, it would be impossible both practically and logically, for one to believe in everything contained by the tradition. However, what one is obliged to believe are the basic ideas that make Judaism a distinctive faith. Especially during the Middle Ages, great Jewish thinkers labored to define the principles (*ikkarim*) of Jewish belief in Torah. These efforts should be not viewed as attempts to provide a rigid list of dogmas, but should be understood as exercises aimed at circumscribing the boundaries of Jewish faith. Within these broad boundaries, each Jew is free to choose from a wide variety of expressions of these fundamental Jewish beliefs. Let me elucidate further by an example.

Picture the Torah—Jewish religious tradition—as a huge smorgasbord of ideas. This would, of course, be a kosher smorgasbord. A huge cornucopia of ideas about various issues of Jewish belief—e.g., God, revelation, messiah, afterlife, Jewish law (*halakhah*), etc.—would be represented by various plates on the table. Nonetheless, the table would have parameters, boundaries, limits. Certain foods like ham and lobster could not appear there. If they did, one could not claim it to be a kosher smorgasbord. Similarly, certain ideas could not appear there, e.g., idolatry, polytheism, the belief that Jesus is the messiah and God incarnate, etc. These ideas are beyond the boundaries of the Torah.

One large section of the smorgasbord would contain a wide variety of different kinds of breads. Since there can be no complete meal without bread, each person would be obliged to choose some kind of bread from the choices offered. Similarly, one cannot have a complete Judaism without belief in God. The Torah, i.e., the tradition, provides many different ideas about God and our relationship to God. One cannot believe in each and all of these various ideas about God. One must choose; one must formulate an idea of God from the choices available, and that would constitute one's belief in God. The same would hold true of each component of the meal, i.e., of each of the fundamental ideas of Judaism. After completing the smorgasbord, each person would have a plate made up of the same basic ingredients, yet each plate would be different. Each person would have a plate of Jewish belief, but its configuration would be different from others.

In sum: a Jew, by definition, is one who has chosen Judaism as a belief-system. The Torah provides the menu of that belief system. In this sense, the Jew is obliged to believe in the Torah. The Torah has boundaries, parameters. It is not infinite. But, within those parameters, there is a plethora of choices. One is obliged to make choices from the options offered. In other words, before one can make choices within Judaism, one must first choose, i.e., commit, to Judaism. One is obliged to learn about Judaism to be able to make informal choices within Judaism. From the choices offered by the Torah, one is obliged to formulate one's own individual, particular configuration of Jewish belief. This process is both active and passive. One accepts the Torah, and from that which one accepts, one is obliged—if one takes Judaism seriously—to actively compose one's own Jewish belief-system. As the talmudic rabbis put it, from the wealth of inherited tradition, from the Torah, one should "derive flour from wheat, a garment from flax."

Byron L. Sherwin, Vice-President
Spertus College of Judaica
Chicago, Illinois

Which Bible Stories Really Happened?

Every Bible story really happened. The people who lived those stories, or who saw the events in the stories, or who heard first-hand accounts of the stories, were struck by the power of God's presence in the events as they unfolded. As they told and retold these stories, they emphasized their sense of awe by highlighting the evidence of God's "unseen hand" in the remarkable (and, sometimes, common) elements of the narrative.

For thousands of years, people were much more concerned with *why* things happened than with *how* things happened. The stories in the Bible may be less exacting in detail about the facts of history than they are about the lessons of history. In fact, details which seem irrelevant or superfluous in the way the Bible tells a story may have been the key to understanding what our ancestors found so important in a given event, much in the same way that we can communicate an entire context to a modern story by placing it in New York, Los Angeles, or Milwaukee—a context which might be lost on a reader from another country or another time in history.

To deny the truth of any story in the Bible is to call into question every story in the Bible, which, ultimately, calls into question the claim of the Jewish people to a covenant with God. To doubt certain aspects of biblical stories, or the lessons one can learn from them, is good fodder for midrash, and in the best of our tradition. The wonderful thing about the Bible is the unlimited learning which can be gleaned from it.

Kids know how it is. The vase in the living room is broken. Did it break because Joey pushed Miriam? Did it break because Miriam was chasing Joey? Did it break

Every Bible story really happened. The people who lived those stories, or who saw the events in the stories, or who heard first-hand accounts of the stories, were struck by the power of God's presence in the events as they unfolded.

because a truck rumbled past the house and knocked it off the shelf? Did it break because "a man came in the window . . ."? The vase is broken. The lessons from its breaking and from the stories told about how it happened may change— but the basic facts do not.

Jack Moline, Rabbi
Agudus Achim Congregation
Alexandria, Virginia

Which Bible Stories Really Happened?

Before we can address the actual question of which Bible stories really happened, the adult (responding to a child's question) must address the issue personally. Adults who aren't comfortable with their own beliefs will not be able to explain it to a child convincingly.

Bible stories bring children more than the mere details of an exciting adventure (Jonah's whale, Noah's ark, Samson's strength), they bring a moral teaching, an ethical understanding and in many cases an example from which children can draw parallels (as remote as they might be) to their own lives. Some of the "truths" our children glean from stories told to them as young children must be "untaught" years later (for example, children perceiving that their God is a bearded king sitting on a throne wearing flowing white robes). This should be factored in, or considered, when we engage in follow-up discussions with children after the story has been read/explained.

Should a child ask whether a specific story happened, a successful approach might be to ask the child what he/she believes. "Do you think that really happened?"

Our children are exposed to high-powered graphics and special effects daily. In fables, legends, and stories they usually formulate an opinion as to whether it actually happened or whether it was make-believe. We should call upon our children's imagination and intuitive resources to determine whether they think it was true. The reality of whether it was true or not is not the crucial issue; because we don't know, and we don't want to be guilty of miseducating and later unteaching what could be perceived as truth. We lose credibility if we teach something as "gospel," and, then as our children pass through stages of development, they

> Should a child ask whether a specific story happened, a successful approach might be to ask the child what he/she believes. "Do you think that really happened?"

learn that we told them things now perceived as untruths. Use the story as the beginning of a discussion based on values. To the persistent child who must know how you feel, you might respond: "This was a wonderful story but I'm not sure it happened." Leaving the child the freedom again to make his/her own selection.

Jack L. Sparks, Educator
Central Synagogue
New York, New York

Were Adam and Eve Really the First People?

The story in the Bible about Adam and Eve gives the reader the impression that they were the first people in the whole world. From what we know today about the origins of human beings, it is highly unlikely that Adam and Eve were the first humans. Our species evolved over many millions of years. The very first humans did not look as we do today. The first people were probably far removed from what we think of as people.

Of course the story is in the Bible to teach us a lesson. It is unimportant whether it is actually a true story or not. Our Jewish tradition wants us to read about Adam and Eve and see in them examples for us today. The story of Adam and Eve helps us see where human beings fit in with all of creation, helps us see aspects of what it may mean to be male and female, helps us try to understand some aspects of family life.

Because the Bible is written in such a way that we do not get all the details we would expect if we were reading a storybook, the rabbis of our tradition try to fill in the blanks and explain the stories. The Adam and Eve portion of the Bible is a favorite story for the rabbis' interpretations. They are able to see all kinds of lessons for us to learn by studying this story. I will share three of them with you.

According to the rabbis, God took dust from the four corners of the earth. God took an equal amount of red dust, then black, then white, then some yellow. God mixed all of this dust with water from all the oceans to indicate that all races are to be included in the first man and none are to be counted as superior over the other.

Another story of the rabbis asks this question: why did God create only a single person, Adam, rather than several

Though modern science tells us that our first ancestors were most likely not Adam and Eve, we still can learn many lessons from the story. It is these lessons that may be considered "truth."

people in the beginning? They answer: so we will know that when one person is destroyed, killed, it is as if the entire world were destroyed. And if one person is saved, it is as if an entire world were saved.

The rabbis ask: why does the Bible say "in the day that God created *a* man on earth"? Because we are to learn that we are to act as good Jews, good human beings, as if we were the only person on earth.

The Adam and Eve story is interesting. Though modern science tells us that our first ancestors were most likely not Adam and Eve, we still can learn many lessons from the story. It is these lessons that may be considered "truth."

Samuel Joseph, Professor of Jewish Education
Hebrew Union College-Jewish Institute of Religion
Cincinnati, Ohio

Why Did Abraham Decide to Be Jewish?

Abraham is, in many ways, one of the more mysterious characters in the Torah. We know virtually nothing of his life before he responded to God's call. The Torah only tells us that he left his native land, Ur, with his father, Terah, his wife, Sarai, and his nephew, Lot, and that they settled in Haran. After his father died, God told Abraham to leave his native land and his father's home and go to the land that God would show him (Genesis 12:1-2).

If we could pinpoint the moment in which Abraham "decided to be Jewish," I think it would be when he answered that call. But what does it mean to say that Abraham became Jewish? Judaism, as we know it, did not yet exist. In fact, the whole Torah (and Jewish teachings ever since) teaches about the evolution of Judaism, which first begins with Abraham. Abraham was not even called a Jew, he was called a Hebrew—"Jew" and "Judaism" are much later terms.

So, what was Abraham before and what did he become? We have learned from studying various historical and archaeological sources that the other peoples who lived in his time worshipped many gods. Most probably, Abraham was raised in a home of polytheists. According to rabbinic legend, in fact, Abraham's father was an idol maker! When Abraham responded to God's call, he chose to separate himself from his people by becoming a monotheist, by worshipping one God.

We don't know why Abraham made this choice. We can only imagine that his reasons may have been similar to those of many people who choose Judaism today. Perhaps Abraham was open to hearing God's call because he was already searching for something different from the religion

By responding to God's call, Abraham embarked on a journey with an unknown destination, without knowing what would be demanded of him along the way. Ultimately, it was his belief in God, his faith that following God's call was the right thing for him to do, that motivated him to "decide to be Jewish."

91

in which he was raised, which held no meaning for him. Believing that there is only one God must have made sense to Abraham and helped him to better understand the world around him and his place in that world. Abraham must have believed that his life would be enriched by heeding God's call.

The promises God made to Abraham gave him direction and a sense of purpose: his descendants would become a great nation, he would be blessed and, in turn, become a blessing to all the nations of the earth.

By responding to God's call, Abraham embarked on a journey with an unknown destination, without knowing what would be demanded of him along the way. Ultimately, it was his belief in God, his faith that following God's call was the right thing for him to do, that motivated him to "decide to be Jewish."

Renni S. Altman, Director
Task Force on the Unaffiliated
Union of American Hebrew Congregations
New York, New York

Why Did Abraham Decide to Be Jewish?

Rabbinic legend tells us that Abraham, as a young boy, worked for his father, Terah, who owned an idol shop. One day, while his father was absent from the store, Abraham took an ax and smashed all the idols except one, the very biggest. In this idol's hands the youth placed the ax. When his father saw the damage done to his place of work, he cried, "Who has done this?"

Abraham answered. "Father, the idols were hungry, and I brought them food. The big god took your ax, killed them all, and ate all the food himself."

Terah stared hard at his son. "Abraham, you are mocking me! You know well that idols can neither move nor eat nor perform any act."

Abraham then spoke softly: "Father, let your ears hear what your tongue speaks."

This story reveals the promise of Abraham's life. At an early age Abraham had recognized that idols could not rule over men and women. People should not serve false gods. They should instead worship the one God who speaks to Abraham in the Bible.

Because of Abraham's faithfulness, the Lord rewards him, as we read in the Bible: "Abraham will become a great and mighty nation, and all the nations of the earth shall be blessed through him. For I have singled him out, that he may teach his children and his children's children to keep the way of the Lord by doing what is just and right" (Genesis 18:18-19).

Because of his faithfulness to his people and his God, Jewish tradition calls Abraham, *Avraham Avinu,* "Abraham, our father." We think of Abraham as the father of the Jewish

At an early age Abraham had recognized that idols could not rule over men and women. People should not serve false gods. They should instead worship the one God who speaks to Abraham in the Bible.

people, but we know that he made the decision to become Jewish, with God's help, while he was still a young boy.

Richard S. Chapin, Associate Rabbi
Congregation Emanu-El of the City of New York
New York, New York

Why Did Abraham Decide to Be Jewish?

As the first of our ancestors, with Sarah, Abraham is often considered to have been the first Jew. However, Abraham did not decide to become a Jew. There simply were no other Jews during Abraham's time whom he could decide to join.

Being the first Jew, Abraham was like an inventor who creates something new in the world. Others who come after the inventor can choose to use the invention or not, can copy or modify it, and can extend its use in ways the original inventor never dreamed of. But the inventor is the first to imagine a new way of doing something. Abraham was a religious inventor with a special talent for walking a new path in relationship with God. It is a path that Jews have been exploring and extending in every generation since Abraham. His "invention" has become the special inheritance of the Jewish people. His path is the path we choose and are chosen to follow.

Abraham was uniquely open to the experience of God. The Torah tells us that Abraham heard God's voice, talked and even argued with God. God was a real presence in his life. Today we talk about making decisions about moving to a new city, becoming a pianist, or even wearing a green sweater. Abraham's decision was different. He felt *impelled* to respond to God's command. He chose to answer a divine imperative to "go forth from your native land and from your father's house to the land that I will show you" (Genesis 12:1). Without any guarantee of safe arrival, without even knowing the name of his destination, Abraham left his familiar surroundings and set out on an unknown journey. With no reservations he answered, "Here I am."

The question "Why did Abraham decide to become a Jew?" is interesting in itself and may be idiosyncratic to

> Abraham was a religious inventor with a special talent for walking a new path in relationship with God. It is a path that Jews have been exploring and extending in every generation since Abraham.

Jews in late-twentieth-century America. The idea that a person can decide to become a Jew, rather than have that identity as a given characteristic along with nationality or gender, or imposed by the surrounding society, is rare in Jewish history. The openness of American society has meant that, for individual religious identification, choice has gained ascendancy over destiny. In asking why Abraham decided to become a Jew, children may also be asking why *they* should be Jews. As parents and teachers we can only answer that question for our children when we can answer it for ourselves. How do we follow in Abraham's footsteps, choosing to remain Jews and to act on our Jewish identity? How will our children make Abraham's invention their own? This is our real challenge.

Dru Greenwood, Director
Commission on Reform Jewish Outreach
Union of American Hebrew Congregations
New York, New York

Did God Really Part the Red Sea?

The Torah teaches us that when Moses and the Jewish people reached the Red Sea, God caused an east wind to blow creating a pathway through which they could cross the sea. The shallow Red Sea, through the force of tide and winds, often is pushed back creating dry pathways. Yet this was a special moment. It was a moment in which the Jewish people felt totally bereft; in that very natural act of wind and tide we experienced God's redemptive power.

Did God part the Red Sea? The Red Sea parted, and in that act our people experienced and understood God's power. I believe that in that crucial moment God's saving power entered the world. At the very moment of despair and hopelessness, a natural act occurred filled with God's presence. These natural acts occur often but only at special times do we feel God's presence involved in our lives. This presence can only be felt when we are ready—and they *were* ready. At this unique moment God met us, and in an extraordinary act we were saved.

Sheldon Zimmerman, Senior Rabbi
Temple Emanuel
Dallas, Texas

The Red Sea parted, and in that act our people experienced and understood God's power. I believe that in that crucial moment God's saving power entered the world.

Did God Really Part the Red Sea?

It might be that in our day and age, miracles have been dismissed as supernatural and unscientific. However, one biblical sense of the word "miracle" is that of a wonder-filled, amazing phenomenon. And even in our technologically based, super-scientific age, wonder and amazement still exist.

What a wonder-filled question! Imagine: our ancestors are fleeing from Pharaoh and his army. Running as fast as they can, carrying all of their possessions, they stay just far enough ahead of Pharaoh to be safe. Then they reach a dead end. A sea stretches before them and there seems to be no way to cross it. Imagine the panic that rushes through the hearts and souls of our great-, great-, great-... grandmothers and grandfathers; they are trapped. In a matter of moments they will be brutally attacked by the pursuing army ... unless something wonder-filled happens.

And it does. Just as Pharaoh and his army are about to reach our ancestors, the waters of this expansive sea part, and our ancestors find a way to cross to the other side in safety. Standing on the far side of the sea, they watch anxiously as Egyptian charioteers and horsemen attempt to follow. If they cross the sea successfully, our ancestors are doomed. And they know it. But, somehow, an amazing thing happens: the Egyptians lose their way. They cannot seem to find the same path which our ancestors used, and they fall into the depths of the sea. Our ancestors are saved.

If you had been there with our ancestors, how could you have watched what happened and not said: "Wow!" Maybe, today, we have trouble explaining what happened there at the shores of the sea. We cannot seem to explain exactly how our ancestors crossed the sea safely while the Egyptian armies did not. Yet our sense of amazement about the event remains. It is this sense of amazement that marks the occurrence of a miracle.

Very often, the Hebrew word used for "miracle" is *neis*. There are, however, other words used in the Bible to denote a miracle. When our ancestors crossed the sea, they exclaimed: "Who is like you, Adonai, among the mighty?

Who is like you, majestic in holiness, awesome in splendor, *oseh feleh*!" (Exodus 15:11). The Hebrew words *oseh feleh* referring to Adonai, literally mean "doing wonder-filled things." It might be that in our day and age, miracles have been dismissed as supernatural and unscientific. However, one biblical sense of the word "miracle" is that of a wonder-filled, amazing phenomenon. And even in our technologically based, super-scientific age, wonder and amazement still exist.

Children, especially in the early to middle primary grades, are very much attuned to wonder and amazement. That is a universally accepted truth among child development theorists. Our children see so many phenomena which evoke an exclamation of "wow" from their lips. Every "wow" is a wonder-filled moment and a miraculous event.

So, how do you respond to a child who asks you if God really parted the Red Sea? I would advise you to encourage your child's natural sense of wonder, and help him/her to imagine the event taking place. If you are comfortable with a theistic conception of God, then describe the amazing intervention of our God in the history of our people. Speak of God as the redeemer in the lives of our ancestors, just as now God is a redeemer and protector in our own lives too. Don't worry so much about a scientific-sounding explanation so much as with nurturing the natural sense of awe, wonder, and fantasy which your child possesses at this age.

If, however, your conception of God is more naturalistic than supernaturalistic, then you might speak to your child of God as the source of the great wonders of our universe: the cosmic energies that erupt in bolts of lightning across a darkened sky; the biological powers that cause flowers to grow from seeds; the emotional urges that arouse your love for someone else. Each of these is evidence of that power which some call God. Similarly, the confluence of natural phenomena which caused the sea to part is evidence of a universe which radiates the power of Adonai.

Abraham Joshua Heschel, the great twentieth-century Jewish philosopher, once cautioned that "as civilization advances, the sense of wonder declines ... mankind will not perish for want of information; but only for want of appreciation." He said that what we lack "is not a will to believe but a will to wonder." In responding to your child's question, you might wish to help him/her retain the gift of wonder.

Steven M. Rosman, Rabbi
Jewish Family Congregation
South Salem, New York

Does God Talk to Me Like God Spoke to Moses?

Jewish tradition has always given Moses a very special place among the prophets and teachers of Israel. The Torah itself ends by speaking of him in this way: "Never again did there arise in Israel a prophet like Moses—whom the Lord singled out, face-to-face" (Deuteronomy 34:10). The phrase "face-to-face" suggests that God spoke to him directly. It does not necessarily mean that God had a face that could be seen, because we know from elsewhere in the Torah that Moses' request to see God is denied: "You cannot see My face, for man may not see Me and live" (Exodus 33:20).

Another famous passage in the Torah clarifies why Moses was unique and tells us a little more about how God may have spoken to him. Miriam and Aaron spoke against Moses and claimed that God also spoke through them to Israel. We are then told that God addressed all three saying: "When a prophet of the Lord arises among you, I make Myself known to him in a vision, I speak with him in a dream. Not so with My servant Moses; he is trusted throughout My household. With him I speak mouth-to-mouth, plainly and not in riddles, and he beholds the likeness of the Lord" (Numbers 12:6-8). It seems that God communicates with other prophets in an obscure and symbolic way, through the images we associate with dreams and trance-like visions. But God was not obscure with Moses, speaking plainly and not in riddles. In addition, the passage suggests that Moses knew more about what God was really like than any other human being, almost like one friend knows another. That is probably why it says he is trusted throughout God's household. When one person knows another person that well, he can understand intuitively what the other one has in mind. In fact, he can even explain what the

Jewish tradition has always given Moses a very special place among the prophets and teachers of Israel. The Torah itself ends by speaking of him in this way: "Never again did there arise in Israel a prophet like Moses—whom the Lord singled out, face-to-face" other person means to others. Perhaps it is in the same way that Moses could speak for God just as though God were speaking through His own mouth. That is probably what is meant by the phrase that God spoke to him "mouth-to-mouth." When people have known each other for a long time and have gone through many experiences together, they can sometimes speak to and for one another in this way.

In the Middle Ages a consensus arose among Jewish thinkers which distinguished Moses from all other prophets and from all other people generally in terms of their different religious experiences. (1) God spoke to Moses directly, but to all others *only* through an intermediary of some kind; (2) God spoke to Moses only when he was fully awake, but to others only in dreams or trancelike visions, if He spoke at all; (3) God spoke to Moses without his ever becoming frightened or confused, while other prophets were usually both frightened and confused because of their experience; and (4) God and Moses could speak with each other whenever either one of them wished, but with others only when God wished (Maimonides, *Mishneh Torah*, Hilkhot Yesodei Ha-Torah 7:6).

All of these descriptions from Jewish tradition suggest that God does not speak with any of us in the way that God spoke with Moses. Still, there is a certain sense in which God *does* speak to us as He spoke to Moses. It has nothing to do with the way in which God speaks—"face-to-face" or "mouth-to-mouth"—but rather with what God has to say. According to our tradition, all of the commandments and teachings that God conveyed to Moses were given to all of the people of Israel, not just in his generation but in every generation. Both God and Moses saw the need for a special people to care about and stand up for God and the things that are most important to God. The commandments and teachings of Jewish tradition, whether they come from Moses' time or later times, are all meant to teach us how to be just and fair with each other, how to worship the one God who represents all things true and good, and how to live in a holy way. Only a community that understands and lives by these kinds of rules can hope to be special enough to endure throughout all of history.

Even when Moses was denied the chance to see God's face, he was nonetheless given all the knowledge necessary to help keep this special community and its ideals alive. Part of the knowledge that Moses gained has come down to us in the Torah's commandments and the traditions about what they mean. Whenever we study them, we should understand that God is speaking to us just as He spoke to Moses about keeping them. Whenever we fulfill them, we should understand that we are at the same time fulfilling the dream of both God and Moses—to be part of a community that will always represent what God cares about most. So while God does not speak to us *in the same way* that He spoke to Moses, He always speaks to us about *the same ideals and obligations* that were part of God's communication with Moses.

Barry S. Kogan, Professor of Jewish Philosophy
Hebrew Union College-Jewish Institute of Religion
Cincinnati, Ohio

Does God Talk to Me Like God Spoke to Moses?

God *can* speak to us as God spoke to Moses. As Martin Buber wrote in *I and Thou*, the great revelations that stand at the beginning of the world's religions are not essentially different in kind from the revelations that happen every day.

The answer to this question will depend, first of all, on what we believe Moses experienced. Did Moses actually see a bush in flame and hear a voice speak out of it as one person speaks to another? On Sinai, did he truly behold God as he ate and drank (Exodus 24:11)? If we take these things literally, we probably have to say no, God no longer talks to people in these ways. The miracles that occurred frequently in biblical times seem in short supply today, and when people *do* think God speaks to them, other people generally perceive them as crazy.

But let us say that we cannot understand Moses' experience literally, that God is not a person and does not hold conversations, though God is everywhere present in the world around us. Let us say that Moses had a profound experience of God's presence, that he felt himself called in a way he could not avoid, that he was addressed, that demands were made on him and he had to respond. To communicate to others the frightening and wonderful things that happened to him, he had to use our everyday human language—even though that language could never entirely convey his experience or say what he wanted to say.

If we take this second view, as I do, then God *can* speak to us as God spoke to Moses. As Martin Buber wrote in *I and Thou*, the great revelations that stand at the beginning of the world's religions are not essentially different in kind from the revelations that happen every day. Certain periods in human history are ready to hear and respond to revelation in ways others are not. But the signs of address are all around us. All the time, through the ordinary events and relationships that make up our lives, God is calling us to the particular task that is ours.

The problem is that generally we have our receivers turned off. Moses saw a burning bush and knew that he was commanded to go and liberate his people. Because we live in a society that discourages us from seeing the world in religious terms, we see a burning bush and reach for a fire extinguisher.

It is not that each of us could be a Moses. Moses was a man of extraordinary religious perception and feeling—and a man who was willing to stake his whole life on his understanding of God's command. But each of us can hear the revelation that is meant for us. Maybe the question is not whether God talks to us but whether we know how to listen, and whether we would put aside our plans, hesitations, and excuses to respond to the call.

Judith Plaskow, Professor of Religious Studies
Manhattan College
Riverdale, New York

Does God Talk to Me Like God Spoke to Moses?

God *does* talk to us in the same way that God talked to Moses. Unfortunately, most of us aren't sure how to listen to God.

God *does* talk to us in the same way that God talked to Moses. Unfortunately, most of us aren't sure how to listen to God. The main cause for misunderstanding is that God doesn't talk to people in the human "mouth-to-ear" kind of talking. How does God talk? Here are some of the ways:

In the Bible, God sometimes spoke to prophets by way of dreams and visions.

God sometimes speaks to us with thoughts and ideas. When an artist or scientist gets a great idea or theory, we say they are *inspired*. The word "inspiration" originally meant that God *breathed in* the idea to us.

In the Bible, God talks to Elijah by way of a "still, small voice" (1 Kings 19:12). This quiet voice was Elijah's conscience.

God speaks through the good actions of people. People are God's language. Sometimes people do special things to help other people without even thinking about why. This is God talking.

God talks to us through the beauty, wonder, and majesty of nature. Sometimes, when people are in the mountains or at the ocean or near large animals or in the desert, they get a tingling feeling, and they can't put their experience into words. This experience is the realization of *Kedushah*, the holiness that we are blessed with. This too is an important way that God speaks to us.

God spoke to Moses, and God speaks to each of us with the Torah. It is said, "Turn it over and over, all can be found in it." Torah contains visions and dreams, thoughts and ideas, the "still small voice" of conscience, good deeds, and holiness. The messages of the Torah are as strong and valid today as they were when God first "spoke" them to Moses.

If we want to hear God talking to us, we have to listen. God speaks silently, to our minds and our hearts.

The most important letter in the Torah is the *alef. Alef* is the first letter of the Ten Commandments *and* the first letter of the Hebrew word for "God." But *alef* is a silent letter. One midrash (in Zohar II:85b) says that the entire Torah is contained in this silent letter. To hear a silent letter, we must listen *very carefully*.

Steven E. Steinbock
author of Torah: The Growing Gift

CHAPTER IV

What About Death and Evil?

1. Why can't the world be perfect?

2. Why do people have to die?

3. Where do people go after they die?

4. Why can't there be peace all the time?

5. Why do some people hate Jews?

6. Why did Hitler kill the Jews?

7. Why are bad people in the world?

8. Why do I sometimes do bad things?

Good and evil, war and peace, pain and pleasure are among the very real opposing forces which do battle in our lives. While some young children may not be aware of war and peace, all are very cognizant of good and evil, pain and pleasure. As they grow, they come to understand about consequences. Some of the things they do engender pleasure, while others yield pain. At times they do something which parents and others praise as good, and at other times they do things for which they are scolded. As they grow, the purpose of their questions changes. When once they persisted in questions beginning with "what" they come to ask questions which begin with "why." Most adults would agree that the "what" questions are often easier to answer than the "why" questions. That is true especially when the topics are good and evil, pain and suffering, war and peace.

While the Torah text tells us that we are essentially good, and the prayerbook tells us that our souls are pure, we know that we often act in ways that are harmful and hurtful. Why? In Deuteronomy we discover that God has granted us the ability to make choices about everything, even life and death: "I have set before you life and death, the blessing and the curse; therefore, choose life." We human beings are free to choose and free to act. Neither God nor fate nor destiny nor the "stars" compels us to act one way or another. We make our own choices. Our actions are our responsibility, not God's or the universe's.

Our choices, however, are made more complicated by the circumstances of our lives, the state of our psyches, and by two impulses which pull and tug at us: the good or benevolent drive (*yetzer tov*) and the bad or "id-like" drive (*yetzer hara*). The rabbis believed that these impulses were contesting one another constantly for conquest of our judgment. It is up to us, they taught, to harness the *yetzer hara* in order to act justly and ethically.

Just as it is up to us to harness the evil impulse in ourselves, so it is also up to us to harness the evil we perceive in society. At times, the existence of pain and suffering in a community is related to the silence of people who could choose to oppose it but do not. Just as the rabbis taught that the performance of a mitzvah leads to another mitzvah, the performance of an *aveirah* (transgression) leads to another *aveirah*. In other words, hate and evil can be contagious. Humankind must take responsibility for the presence of evil, pain, and suffering which we perceive and choose to ignore. God is not to be blamed for evil which human beings perpetrate against other human beings. It is our fault.

Whereas some instances of evil clearly might result from our choices, other evils are tougher to explain. Job's demands for an answer to the evils of his suffering are not satisfactorily explained. In fact, God responds from out of the whirlwind that the ways of the Divine often are incomprehensible to the limited human intellect: "Then how can you say My ways are wrong or condemn Me in order to justify yourself? Are you in any fashion like God? Can you rule the world in majesty?" Indeed, the rabbis concurred that there are times when explaining "the relative peace of the wicked and the suffering of the righteous is beyond us."

Surely, to the extent that we are able it is important to understand the reasons for what we perceive to be good and evil, pain and pleasure, war and peace, and teach our children. One caveat though: Judgments like good and bad ought to be weighed very carefully before they are attached to people instead of to the deeds people perform. If children sense that people who do good things are automatically considered good people and people who do bad things are automatically considered bad people, then there is a danger that they will apply the same labels to themselves, especially when they do things which might be considered bad.

Someone once observed that guilt is the result of feeling badly about what one has done, and shame is the result of feeling badly about who one is. Shame is a threat to self-esteem and healthy growth. So, when talking about matters of good and evil with children, it is important to help them understand that Jewish tradition teaches that all people are born with pure souls, that people are free to make choices and must take responsibility for the choices they make and accept the consequences of those choices, and that some choices lead to healthy and benevolent acts, while others lead to harmful and hurtful acts.

Why Can't the World Be Perfect?

I believe that God could have created a perfect world, a world in which every one of us would be programmed always to do the right thing. In such a world, there would be no murder, no war, no lying, no hurting other people. But in such a world, there would be no goodness, because nobody would be *choosing* to be good.

We human beings are different from all other living creatures because all other creatures are controlled by instinct while we can choose what we want to do. This means that we are free to choose wrongly and do things that hurt ourselves and others. Animals can be inconvenient or disobedient but they can't be bad, because only human beings are responsible for what they choose to do.

But it also means that only we are free to choose to do the *right* thing. As the Talmud says, "when a person chooses to do something right when he doesn't have to, God looks down and says, 'For this moment alone it was worth creating the world.'"

I believe that God could have created a perfect world, a world in which every one of us would be programmed always to do the right thing. In such a world, there would be no murder, no war, no lying, no hurting other people. But in such a world, there would be no goodness, because nobody would be *choosing* to be good. And I think that maybe God loves goodness even more than He loves perfection. The word "perfect" doesn't only mean "flawless, nothing wrong." It also means "finished, complete." A perfect world would be like a completed jigsaw puzzle. It would be very pretty to look at, but it wouldn't be fun or challenging any more.

Sometimes we see life as less than perfect because we let ourselves care about things and about people who are vulnerable to injury and accident. People we love grow old and die. Things we love fall and break. But we would be a lot less human than we are if we were afraid to love because loving opened us up to being hurt. So we just have to be brave and accept the imperfections of the world, and the pain that comes from daring to love.

I suspect that all of this theological explanation isn't very comforting when something has gone terribly wrong in your life, when someone you care about is sick or something you thought you deserved doesn't work out the way you hoped it would. To be told that the world is better for not being perfect doesn't cheer you up much. All I can say to you then is that I believe God is just as sad as you are that the world is so often unfair. He has taught us what we need to know to be good, and He has promised to be with us to keep us strong and brave in this less-than-perfect world.

Harold S. Kushner, Rabbi Emeritus
Temple Israel
Natick, Massachusetts

Why Can't the World Be Perfect?

Joseph realizes that the world is not perfect or imperfect, but that it is a mystery. He understands that he will never know the true meaning of the events in the world. In his old age he is like a child, full of wide-eyed curiosity, openness, and wonder about life.

A story:

Once when Joseph was a boy, he was alone with Jacob, his father. All his brothers had taken their flocks to a distant pasture. Worried about the welfare of his other sons, or perhaps wishing Joseph to be included in their work, Jacob sent Joseph off to visit them.

Arriving at the place where his brothers are supposed to be, Joseph discovers that they have moved on. But he meets a man in the field who is able to direct him. When he joins his brothers, he is soon the victim of their plot against him and is thrown in a pit and then sold into slavery.

I imagine Joseph thinking of the man in the field and wishing he had never met him. At this moment Joseph knows the world is not perfect, for he feels abandoned and frightened.

Joseph arrives in Egypt and quickly rises in power and prestige. He is a man of great authority and comfort. He recalls the man in the field and realizes that had it not been for him, he would not be in such a promising place. The world may not be perfect, Joseph decides, for he has been wounded by his brothers and misses his home, but it's pretty good.

Soon after this, Joseph is unjustly accused and is thrown into prison. He is there for years. In his darkest moments, he thinks of the man in the field with bitterness. From his prison cell the world looks cruel. Not only does he have his old family wounds and longings, but he feels he will die forgotten in this darkness.

Joseph is released from prison and, through his ability to interpret dreams, achieves a position of princely influence in Egypt. Due to his foresight and good management, he is able to protect the country from starvation. Thousands of people come to receive grain from him during the famine. Joseph feels blessed to be able to help others, and in his heart he thanks the man in the field: through him a whole nation is being aided in its time of need. Life, he muses, does have a strange kind of perfection and a great beauty. In his maturity Joseph is beginning to understand how different the world looks depending on where you are and what you are experiencing.

The famine causes people from distant places to come for help, and among them one day appear the members of Joseph's own family, the very brothers who betrayed him. Old wounds open with anger and sorrow. With a pang Joseph thinks again of the man in the field. Because of that man, a strange and painful destiny begins.

But through his meetings with his brothers, he finally comes to terms with his hurt. The love he bears them and his father rises to the surface of his heart. He forgives them. He shares a great reunion, blessed by his father and accepted by his kin.

On the day when he buries his father Jacob, Joseph thinks again about the man in the field he met so many years ago. He marvels at the strange course of his life, how there were times when he felt like the king of a perfect world, and other times when he felt he was the lowest outcast. Joseph realizes that the world is not perfect or imperfect, but that it is a mystery. He understands that he will never know the true meaning of the events in the world. In his old age he is like a child, full of wide-eyed curiosity, openness, and wonder about life. Yet, unlike a child, he knows that after all the questions have been answered, life will still be a mystery.

At last the time comes for his own death. Lying on his bed, with his life fading, Joseph has a vision. He is a young man walking down a road; the road ends at the edge of a field; the field becomes a garden. In this garden he sees his father, his mother, his ancestors back through thirty generations. They are all there in a great circle, and there also, coming toward him, is the man of the field, the very same man who once showed him the way to his brothers. But now he is radiant with a light that is not earthly, and with outstretched hands, the man welcomes Joseph to Paradise.

Peter Pitzele, Director of Psychodrama Services
Four Winds Hospital
Katonah, New York

Why Do People Have to Die?

What an important and thoughtful question. I bet everybody has asked that question at one time or another. It's frightening (for everyone) to know that people you love won't always be with you. It's frightening to know that you, too, will someday die.

When children pose the question, try to determine what they really want to know, as well as their motivation. Are they asking for reassurance? Are they curious about what happens to a person's body when he or she dies? Are they questioning God? It is all too easy to misinterpret this important question. Too often adults get involved in a deep theological discussion when youngsters are really striving to understand the biological processes of dying and death. It's like the old story of the child who asks, "Where do I come from?" The parents then proceed to give a lengthy sexual explanation, when all the child really wanted to know was if she came from Boston or Baltimore.

In my experience, I have found that children can most readily understand the mystery of death through an explanation of nature. For example, water has various forms: rain, snow, ice, lakes, oceans, streams, geysers, glaciers, waterfalls. There are changes and growth each day—of larva to butterfly, egg to tadpole and frog. New leaves replace old ones that die.

Adults may say to children, "Look in the woods. See those plants that are dying? Soon they will die. But look here. Other shoots are beginning to come up." Adults can stress that nature constantly renews itself; it is the same for people. Living and dying is part of human unfolding. All things have a life span—our bodies, trees, flowers, animals, and plants. Biologists tell us that everything that is alive is

When children pose the question, try to determine what they really want to know, as well as their motivation. Are they asking for reassurance? Are they curious about what happens to a person's body when he or she dies? Are they questioning God?

the renewal of something that died. These are the cyclic rhythms of nature—night and day, phases of the moon, seasons, lives of insects, seeds, plants, animals, and people.

Judaism teaches that death is terribly sad and painful; but it is also an essential part of life: "There is a time to be born and a time to die" (Ecclesiastes 3:2). We are as "a wind that passes and comes not again" (Psalm 78:39). "For what person can live and never see death?" (Psalm 89:49). And from the very first book of the Bible, "You are dust and to dust you shall return" (Genesis 3:19).

Some children may be questioning God when they ask, "Why do people have to die?" Let children know that no one knows. But most of us can agree on one thing—that death adds a vital dimension to living. An awareness of our limited days on earth makes it more urgent that we be at our best— that we must really *live*. Death makes the value of life more imperative—not in the sense of being morbidly preoccupied with thoughts of dying, but in living life. The personal tragedy lies not in what we might do with our brief existence on earth, but in what we might not do—the love we fail to give, the efforts we give up on, the kindness we neglect to bestow. We must do our best in the face of the fact that we all must die. We all must strive to make each day more meaningful!

Let children know that Judaism is not only concerned with the hereafter, but with the here and now. A Jewish student once asked, "If you heard that the Messiah was coming, and you were planting a tree, what should you do?" Her wise teacher replied, "First plant the tree. Then see if the Messiah is coming." In other words, in the face of death, L'Chaim (to life)!

Earl A. Grollman, Rabbi Emeritus
Beth El Temple Center
Belmont, Massachusetts

Where Do People Go After They Die?

To ask the question "Why do people have to die?" is to venture into the very depths of our understandings about life and about human nature. Centuries of Jewish thought offer us two basic answers to the question.

The first answer is that death exists in general, and that people die in particular, because they have sinned. The idea is biblical (Genesis 3:22-24). Adam and Eve sinned. As punishment God deprived them of their potential immortality. The ancient rabbis picked up on that idea: "There is no death without sin" (Babylonian Talmud, Shabbat 55a).

I would *reject* this notion and would not teach it to a child; I believe it might make a child overly obsessive about "sinning," or wrongdoing. It has the potential to create a certain sense of anxiety and fear, and does little to instill a love of God. It is also not true in any verifiable sense. There are a lot of sinners who live to old age and a lot of good people who die young. I would prefer the biblical teaching that God does not require the death of sinners, but that we turn back to God (*teshuvah*).

The second answer is that death is inevitable because it is part of the very fabric of the world. That idea is also biblical: God made humanity from the dust of the earth and to dust we must return (Genesis 2:7, 3:19; Job 10:9). The idea moves easily into the rabbinic period, where we find such statements as the one that the Angel of Death was created on the first day of creation, or another that describes death as being the strongest thing in the world. A rabbinic legend tells us that the angels thought that Adam was a god, until God put him to sleep. Death is what separates us from God. Only God is eternal.

Not only does death separate us from God. It is precisely

Death is inevitable because it is part of the very fabric of the world. That idea is also biblical: God made humanity from the dust of the earth and to dust we must return.

119

death that makes way for new life and for the renewal of creation. Death is part of the natural order. Death *restores* the natural order through the cycle of growth and death and decay. We might even say that there could be no life without death.

I would offer yet a third reflection on death. The presence of death as a natural occurrence guarantees that our lives are worth something. Without death before us as an inevitable end, there would be no impetus to do great things. We would become lazy and do little that is productive; we would be without the belief that a portion of what we do is intended to survive us. We will not live forever. This means that we have to work as hard as we can right now to make ourselves and our world a little bit better. I believe that certain mitzvot that we do create a light within us. It is this light that survives even death.

Jeffrey K. Salkin, Rabbi
Central Synagogue of Nassau County
Rockville Centre, New York

Where Do People Go After They Die?

This question seems to imply that there is a particular place to which people are assigned after death. While traditional Judaism speaks of the Garden of Eden as an abode for the righteous after death, neither its location nor its character is properly defined. There is also a tradition in Judaism that with the coming of the Messiah the righteous dead will be resurrected in the land of Israel and live in an era of universal peace and righteousness. As satisfying as these promises may be for some, many of us are unpersuaded and seek a more rational sense of what happens after death, of what death takes away and what it leaves behind.

Death takes much away! Our physical selves cease to exist. We can no longer share or enjoy physical contact with others. We do not know or think or feel, nor are we aware after death of any of the things of which we had conscious knowledge during our lifetime. To say this, however, does not mean that there is nothing left of us in the world we leave behind.

Our meaning for life and life's meaning for us are not confined to the days of our years. Much of what was most important to us will survive our death as a vital force in the lives of others. Our children, our children's children are an extension of ourselves. Just as the values and the ideals of our lives are a gift from the past, so, too, will the values and ideals of our lives be a gift to the future yet to be lived. Though we do not live in the past, the past can and does live in us. So, too, will we live in the lives and memories of generations yet unborn. As teachers, parents, and friends we impart a share of our being, perhaps the most important part, to others whose lives become a living manifestation of the things most precious to us.

The prophets envisioned that a time will come when peace will prevail, justice will reign, and truth and righteousness will everywhere be found. This time will be a memorial to former generations who lived and died for the Kingdom of God on earth. It will be the assurance of an immortality that we will share because of the lives we will have lived.

William James, a religious thinker, once said, "The greatest use of a life is to spend it for something that outlasts it." The institutions of learning or of worship or of public service to which we give our strength and our time, enable us to continue as a living force in the lives of others, sharpening their minds, strengthening their spirits and easing the burdens of life.

The prophets envisioned that a time will come when peace will prevail, justice will reign, and truth and righteousness will everywhere be found. This time will be a memorial to former generations who lived and died for the Kingdom of God on earth. It will be the assurance of an immortality that we will share because of the lives we will have lived.

Where do people go after they die? They don't go anywhere, they simply *are*, for, as Thomas Campbell once said, "To live in hearts we leave behind is not to die."

Jerome Malino, Rabbi Emeritus
United Jewish Center
Danbury, Connecticut

Where Do People Go After They Die?

To answer the question of where people go after they die, you will need to spend some time with your own feelings about afterlife. Whether a child asks out of simple inquisitiveness or in response to the death of one with whom they shared life, your answer should provide an honesty that will continue to serve them as they grow and mature. Pious platitudes that you do not believe will not long serve a child, and while you must answer in concert with the child's level of understanding, you should avoid expedient simplicities that create fears. Therefore, it is wise to avoid such answers as "Grandpa went to sleep."

In searching through your feelings about afterlife, the traditions of Judaism provide a fairly wide spectrum of options to examine. Before turning to that spectrum, it is important to remember that Judaism's primary focus is on how we live in this life. Though views of the world-to-come are present throughout Jewish history, they differ widely and are almost always secondary to the issues of life in this world.

Afterlife is generally couched in the framework of *olam ha-ba*, literally "the world-to-come." Judaism has a significant amount of terminology related to *olam ha-ba*, but little in the way of authoritative prescription concerning definitions of these terms. The spectrum of views spans from a nebulous picture of an afterlife of physical, emotional, and intellectual existence to an afterlife present only in the hearts and minds of the living. Between these poles, the spectrum passes through various understandings of a transcendent soul.

Judaism's offerings, then, include an existence beyond death where physicality and consciousness continue. In this view we see a hazily pictured Garden of Eden, where

To answer the question of where people go after they die, you will need to spend some time with your own feelings about afterlife. Whether a child asks out of simple inquisitiveness or in response to the death of one with whom they shared life, your answer should provide an honesty that will continue to serve them as they grow and mature.

harmony and well-being are the norm and people bask in God's blessing.

Alternatively, we are offered the view that, despite the loss of physicality, the soul, the essence of being, continues beyond death. This concept may be manifest in a range from conscious to unconscious states of being; from souls that retain individuality to those that merge into a well of soul material from which new souls are formed.

Or, finally, we are offered the concept that the only life beyond death is that to be found in the hearts, minds, and beings of the living. In life we affect people; when we die the effects of our existence remain. We find "afterlife" in the continuation of what we did, of how we shaped and influenced people and events. Our afterlife exists in the feelings and memories of us carried by the living.

Norman Koch, Rabbi
Temple Sholom
New Milford, Connecticut

Why Can't There Be Peace All the Time?

This question is a little like asking "Why can't I just get straight A's all the time?" It takes a lot of hard work and a great deal of preparation and diligence to get the best grades. Peace is not obtainable just because everybody wants it. It actually is a process of *negotiating, compromising and making good decisions*. We are always "seeking peace" or "making peace." Perhaps we should coin the term "peacing," for peace is always active like a verb, not static, like a noun.

Amos Oz, the famous Israeli novelist, calls himself a "peacenik." The difference between this and a pacifist is that while he won't fight an aggressive war, he will stand up against others who do so. Judaism is very much a "peacenik" religion, for we are taught: "Seek peace *and* pursue it" (Psalm 34:15). It is by strongly working for peace and always looking for peaceful solutions that we strengthen ourselves. It is out of this moral strength that our tradition also teaches us, "Prepare for battle! Arouse the warriors. Let all the fighters come and draw near!" (Joel 4:9). Sometimes we must fight for peace against aggressors, against abuse of power, and against injustice.

The Talmud describes two types of war: *milchemet mitzvah* (necessary war), which is waged to defend your own country or withstand an aggressor, and *milchemet reshut* (optional war), which is not considered absolutely necessary and therefore is not always justified. The Second World War was considered by many to be a justifiable war because of Hitler's naked aggression against neighboring countries and his crimes against all humanity in perpetrating the Holocaust. Israel's wars against her Arab neighbors have largely been seen in the same way since she was defending her right to exist.

The Hebrew word for "peace," *shalom*, derives from a root meaning completeness. To be at peace means to be complete, to have a unified world; one that manifests justice for all and harmony for all peoples and nations.

The Hebrew word for "peace," *shalom*, derives from a root meaning completeness. To be at peace means to be complete, to have a unified world; one that manifests justice for all and harmony for all peoples and nations. The prophets of Israel envisioned a time when people would "beat their swords into plowshares and their spears into pruning hooks, [when] nation shall not lift up sword against nation. Neither shall they learn war any more. But every man shall sit under his vine and fig tree, and none shall make them afraid" (Micah 4:3-4). This is Judaism's goal for a messianic time. It is a goal that each of us must strive for by pursuing peace in our daily lives.

Michael J. Shire, Director
Centre for Jewish Education
London, England

126

Why Can't There Be Peace All the Time?

God gives each of us the right to make choices. The ability to choose makes a person free. And with the ability to choose also comes conflict. One person's choice may be in conflict with another person's choice. For example, one person wants to study. A second person wants to play loud music. What each person chooses will be in conflict with the other's choice. A conflict will occur unless a compromise of some kind can be agreed upon.

Nations are like people. Because nations are so different from each other, one nation's choice may clash with another nation's choice. For example, when the United Nations was considering the establishment of the State of Israel, the Jews chose to be part of the political decision-making process. On the other hand, the Arabs chose to boycott the proceedings. Both groups made a choice. These choices were in conflict. It is a conflict that continues till today.

Choice is unique to human beings. It is the essence of freedom. Without choice, there is no freedom. Unfortunately, as we know from history, it is not easy for us to make the choice to live free and to live in peace.

It is up to each of us to become a pursuer of peace.

Richard M. Morin, Executive Vice President
National Association of Temple Educators
Nashville, Tennessee

God gives each of us the right to make choices. The ability to choose makes a person free. And with the ability to choose also comes conflict. One person's choice may be in conflict with another person's choice.

127

Why Do Some People Hate Jews?

Hatred comes from ignorance—we counter it by learning about each other.

Almost two thousand years ago there was a major revolution that began in Israel. A new religious belief was started that centered around the life and death of a Jew named Jesus. Those who followed this faith believed that Jesus was a messiah—one who was sent by God to save the world from its pain and suffering. According to the Christian Bible, Jesus was arrested by the Roman authorities as a political prisoner and was sentenced to be put to death as a political insurgent. The ruling authorities, in honor of the approaching holiday, offered to release either Jesus or another prisoner. Those who were in the town square chose to set free the *other* prisoner. Thus, Jesus was put to death by crucifixion, a Roman form of punishment. According to the Christian Bible, Jesus rose from the dead to prove to the world that he was God.

Judaism rejected the belief in Jesus as messiah. Further, as reported in the Christian Bible, the people in the town square were Jews. Therefore, for almost two millennia, Christians despised Jews because of their rejection of the Christian faith and their supposed participation in the death of Jesus. Jews stuck with their own faith—a faith that got them through the hardship of the enslavement in Egypt, the destruction of the First and Second Temples, the expulsion from their land, and countless other tragedies.

It is the way of the world that people take umbrage with those who do not accept the majority position. It is part of human nature to dislike those who are different and refuse to conform. The Jewish people have moved from place to place in every age, holding fast to the faith of their ancestors. It has been our faith that has gotten us through countless challenges to our existence. Ironically, it has been our steadfast insistence on maintaining our faith that has caused many to hate us.

The last twenty-six years have seen a marked change in the attitude the church has held about the Jews. A very positive relationship has developed. It is our hope that in time the hatred will disappear, so that we can work together—and celebrate our differences. Hatred comes from ignorance—we counter it by learning about each other.

Gary M. Bretton-Granatoor, Director
Department of Interreligious Affairs
Union of American Hebrew Congregations
New York, New York

Why Do Some People Hate Jews?

The legacy of hatred against Jews goes back a thousand years, when Christianity became the dominant religion of the Western world.

The legacy of hatred against Jews goes back a thousand years, when Christianity became the dominant religion of the Western world. As Christianity consolidated its power, it subjected the Jews—accused of the murder of Jesus and of stubbornly refusing to accept Christianity—to an ever-expanding policy of isolation and degradation.

Politically, Jews were deprived of their citizenship and their legal and civil rights. They were expelled altogether from England in 1298, France in 1394, and Spain in 1492. In Italy and Germany, where they remained, Jews were forced to wear identifying badges and then were further segregated into ghettos that were locked by a gate at night.

Economically, Jews were forced into more and more marginal activities. In the ninth century they were major international merchants and bankers. By the sixteenth century, they were only allowed to be pawnbrokers and dealers in second-hand clothing.

Socially, interaction between Jews and Christians became more and more violent. The crusaders, on their way to the Holy Land, first attacked the Jews in their midst. Ten thousand Jews died during the First Crusade alone. Starting in the twelfth century, whole Jewish communities were destroyed on the false charge that they had engaged in the ritual murder of Christian children. During the Black Death, when the Jews were maliciously accused of causing the epidemic by poisoning the wells, 350 Jewish communities were destroyed.

The stereotypes of Jews that had their inception in the Middle Ages are still held today. The occupations into which Jews were forced—pawnbroking, dealing in second-hand wares—instilled in the people a picture of the Jew as a manipulator of money and goods, cheating his customer and becoming rich in the process. As Christians became less and less acquainted with Jews because of their expulsion from many European countries and their segregation in ghettos in the rest, fantastic beliefs about Jews circulated freely. Jews were said to be devils with horns, tails, and hoofs who murdered Christian children for their blood and purposely disrupted church services by desecrating the wafer representing the body of Jesus.

With the emancipation of Jews in the nineteenth century, the medieval restrictions against them disappeared, but the legacy of hatred which had been carefully instilled was not forgotten.

Nationalist anti-Semites in various European countries claimed that the Jews were aliens who could never truly become members of the nation. The Russian pogroms against the Jews utilized this calumny, which is now being revived by modern Russian anti-Semites.

Racial anti-Semitism transmuted the religious basis for the hatred of Jews into the new scientific terms of the twentieth Century. The new social sciences classified the various peoples of the world into separate "races," ranking each race in a hierarchy of merit. Jews were placed at the bottom of the hierarchy as a morally and culturally inferior race that had contributed little or nothing to civilization. And the new science of genetics added that in any cross between "inferior" and "superior" races the inferior predominated. The Nazis made this doctrine the cornerstone of their policy. They claimed they had to rid the world of the Jews because otherwise the Jews would intermarry with other Europeans and thus cause the dreadful decay of Western civilization. The result was the Holocaust—the calculated annihilation of six million Jewish men, women, and children, a third of the world's population of Jews.

In the last twenty years, hatred of the Jews has gone through yet another transformation. The passage in 1975 of the United Nations resolution equating Zionism with racism offered anti-Semites a new respectability. Bigots, using the term "Zionism" as a code word for "Jews," challenged the legitimacy of the State of Israel, and denied the right of the Jewish people to a nation of their own.This resolution was repealed in December, 1991.

Today American Jewry is more accepted and secure than Diaspora Jewry has ever been in any other place or time. Laws that guarantee fair housing, employment opportunities and civil rights have made overt forms of institutionalized discrimination against Jews and other minorities illegal.

The Roman Catholic Church and many Protestant denominations have adopted strongly worded theological statements that mark an increased acceptance of Judaism and a rejection of traditional religious anti-Semitism.

Public opinion polls indicate that many of the stereotypes about Jews have markedly declined as America's population has become more worldly and better educated. However, these public opinion surveys also show that as many as one-third of all Americans are still susceptible to anti-Semitic propaganda. They accept as true prejudiced remarks that they hear from their parents, friends, or peers. The polls also show the persistence of hard-core anti-Semites, who constitute approximately 5 percent of the American population. These are the people who produce pamphlets and books claiming a Jewish conspiracy to control the world and who join extremist groups that target synagogues and Jewish organizations for vandalism and desecration.

The annual audits of anti-Semitism by the Anti-Defamation League indicate a yearly average of close to 700 acts of vandalism against Jewish institutions and 400 acts of harassment, threats and assaults against individual Jews. Anti-Semitism on college campuses has risen sharply in the last few years, with graffiti and verbal abuse frequently reported. Some campus speakers and editorial writers spout an anti-Zionist rhetoric that sometimes reflects anti-Semitism, not merely political criticism. Black speakers who are followers of the Nation of Islam blame Jews for many of the ills that blacks suffer in the society.

Some people today still hate Jews, continuing to carry within themselves the seeds of hatred planted so long ago in medieval Europe.

Frances M. Sonnenschein, Director
National Education Department
Anti-Defamation League of B'nai B'rith
New York, New York

Why Do Some People Hate Jews?

Though we may be able to explain all of the political, psychological, and historical reasons for anti-Semitism, we have been unable to eradicate it among humankind. It is unlikely that we can simply make it go away when it threatens the well-being of our children. Still, we can strive to make our children feel protected when they are threatened, loved when they encounter hatred, and proud of their Jewish heritage when they face anti-Semitism.

When a young child asks this question it may be an indication that s/he actually has been victimized by anti-Semitism or has witnessed the victimization of others. This is both sad and troubling. It is discomfiting to be singled out for being different—for any reason. It is absolutely frightening to feel threats or hatred in the taunts or the discriminatory behavior others aim at you. For young children who are still struggling to feel secure in the world of others, persecution is an evil that is truly terrifying.

It is vitally important to take our children's terror seriously, and to help them feel safe and secure. It is equally important for our children to maintain their self-respect and their respect for other people, especially when the integrity and worth of the Jewish people is challenged by slur and malice.

Here is a parable written by Saul Teplitz about what happened once upon a time when a scottie dog encountered anti-scottie dog hatred. Perhaps it might serve as a gentle model for anyone who has been assaulted by hatred and discrimination.

"There was once a scottie dog who found himself lost and alone in a neighborhood of Irish terriers. Every time the scottie walked down the street, the terriers would bark at him in rage. He was quite puzzled and hurt, but instead of wondering what bothered the terriers, he began to analyze himself. Perhaps the terriers barked at him because he was different. He, therefore, tried very hard to be like the terriers. He began to wag his tail as they did and to prick up his ears as they did. He even barked in as perfect an imitation as could be achieved. And still they barked every time he went by.

The scottie then decided to call in experts to write scholarly dissertations which would prove the greatness of the contributions of the scotties to canine civilization. Soon there were mountains of statistics to point up the courage of the scotties through a computation of the number of people they had rescued from burning buildings and drownings. Unfortunately, the only ones that read the books and the statistics were other scotties. Whatever, the scottie continued to bark as in the past. Finally, the scottie decided that since he was a scottie, he had better act like one and live like one, and be the best possible scottie he could be. And if the terriers still barked, there was nothing he could do about it."

Though we may be able to explain all of the political, psychological, and historical reasons for anti-Semitism, we have been unable to eradicate it among humankind. It is unlikely that we can simply make it go away when it threatens the well-being of our children. Still, we can strive to make our children feel protected when they are threatened, loved when they encounter hatred, and proud of their Jewish heritage when they face anti-Semitism.

Steven M. Rosman, Rabbi
Jewish Family Congregation
South Salem, New York

Why Did Hitler Kill the Jews?

The ideas and actions of the Nazis were the culmination of a two-thousand-year history of anti-Semitism.

The simple answer is that Hitler, the Nazis, and their collaborators killed six million Jews because Jewish civilization was and is the antithesis of Nazism. However, this question deserves more than a simple answer.

The ideas and actions of the Nazis were the culmination of a two-thousand-year history of anti-Semitism. Traditions of Jew-hatred emerged from religious and secular sources, from political and economic theories, and in the nineteenth century from a pseudo-scientific racism that became an especially lethal component of Nazism. Taken together, these ideas helped Hitler and his followers use the Jews as scapegoats for Germany's defeat in World War I and subsequent problems. Thus, the subjugation and murder of Jews (as well as the persecution of other "alien" groups, such as gypsies, blacks, homosexuals, the handicapped, and Jehovah's Witnesses) became an important way for the Third Reich to "restore German honor."

The devastation of European and North African Jewry occurred not only because of anti-Semitism, but also because of apathy. The United States rescued far too few of the refugees, Great Britain sealed the gates of Palestine, and many other governments did little to counter the annihilation of the Jews. While Jews and others in occupied countries heroically resisted the Nazis, and although the Allied forces eventually destroyed the Axis powers, these efforts were not sufficient to protect the victims of genocide.

Still, it is important to remember that the Jewish people and heritage survived. Individuals began new lives, families were reunited and built anew, and while countless communities were lost others were reinvigorated, especially in North America and the reborn State of Israel. Nazism was defeated, and some—though too few—of its principal leaders were brought to justice. And the world is left to confront the future with an inescapable imperative to forge hope out of memory.

David Altshuler, Director
A Living Memorial to the Holocaust—
Museum of Jewish Heritage in New York City
New York, New York

Why Did Hitler Kill the Jews?

When Hitler came along, and in speech after speech promised a good new life if only they would get rid of the Jews, people listened.

A verse in a Purim song written by the late Ben Aronin goes:

> Oh, once there was a wicked man
> And Haman was his name, sir.
> He lied and lied about the Jews
> But they were not to blame, sir."

We could substitute Hitler's name and be almost correct. Almost, because Hitler was more than wicked, he was an evil tyrant. A tyrant is like the bully in school who bosses everyone around and beats up people who don't listen to him.

There have been many tyrants in the world who started wars to get more land. More often it was to cover up their country's problems by blaming someone else or another group of people.

There have been other tyrants beside Haman who tried to "boss around" the Jewish people. Antiochus tried to stop us from learning and living as Jews, and Pharaoh enslaved us to build cities and pyramids.

Hitler was the worst tyrant of all. He was a man with great leadership ability. He had such a persuasive way of speaking that people listened even when he told lies. Yet he used his talents for evil. As a child, his violent temper exploded when he didn't get his way. He organized the neighborhood children into gangs to raid apple trees. He could talk them into it even though they knew it was wrong.

As a child, Hitler had dreams of becoming an artist. Despite his tyrannical father's opposition, he dropped out of high school and went to Vienna, hoping to be admitted to the Academy of Fine Arts. He did so badly on the exams that he was refused admission.

Hitler was outraged, became depressed. He didn't seem to care how he lived or dressed. It was in this condition that he met his first Jews. There were 200,000 Jews in Vienna. Hitler claimed in his later writings that he had never met Jews as a child or even heard his parents use the word "Jew." Yet he grew up in a European atmosphere which for nineteen hundred years had been anti-Semitic—blaming the Jews for killing Christ.

Hitler didn't like the appearance of the Eastern European Jews. He was jealous of the established well-to-do Jews. In his sick mind, he began to believe that all of Germany's problems were caused by the Jews.

Germany had been badly defeated in World War I. The country was in ruins. There were no jobs, no money, and prices kept rising. People were looking for a leader to set things right.

When Hitler came along, and in speech after speech promised a good new life if only they would get rid of the Jews, people listened. They eventually believed all his lies about the Jews.

They elected him Chancellor, then President of Germany.

Our Jewish tradition teaches that each person has a *yetzer tov* and a *yetzer hara* inside—the inclination for good or bad. All one of us have to learn to develop the good side of our nature.

Hitler allowed his *yetzer hara* to corrupt his leadership ability—taking a destructive path from the time he assumed power, he started the worst war the world had ever seen, killed six million of our people, destroyed his country once again, and ended by committing suicide.

Yes, Hitler is dead, the Nazi party disbanded.

Other tyrants still appear from time to time, such as Sadam Hussein.

The United States and other democratic countries are continually on the alert to keep them in control.

Each one of us can work to develop our *yetzer tov* and try to build a world *b'shalom*—"in peace."

Marvell Ginsburg, Director
Early Childhood Department
Board of Jewish Education of Metropolitan Chicago
Chicago, Illinois

Why Are Bad People in the World?

My first response is to say that very rarely is there a really bad or evil person in the world. Rather, there are mostly people who choose bad or inappropriate behavior. Maybe they are hurt or angry; maybe they were abused or hurt as children and had no one to teach them how to behave correctly. Sometimes it is greed or selfishness that makes them react in a way that hurts others. Sometimes they are mentally sick and are not able to tell right from wrong. Sometimes they are following what others in a group say and haven't considered the consequences of their actions. Sometimes they are bad in our eyes, but doing what another culture teaches is acceptable.

Jewish tradition teaches that people have to choose life and good over death and evil. Allowing God to be in our lives and listening to the Jewish values in Torah and our other sources helps individuals to know how to choose good and appropriate behavior. Our tradition also says that we have to be *taught* how to be good. Since there is the possibility for human beings to choose either, we must help shape the choices they make.

Yet I also think that every once in a while there is a person who seems to be evil, who likes to hurt others, and who uses his power to do evil in the world. Sometimes I think that this person—like Pharaoh, Amalek, Haman, Torquemada, Stalin, and Hitler—is an example to us of what we can become if we do not strive to choose good and moral behavior. Jewish tradition suggests that God created both light and darkness, good and evil.

> I am the Lord, and there is none else;
> I form the light, and create darkness;
> I make peace, and create evil;
> I am the Lord, that doest all these things.
> (Isaiah 45:7)

Jewish tradition teaches that people have to choose life and good over death and evil. Allowing God to be in our lives and listening to the Jewish values in Torah and our other sources helps individuals to know how to choose good and appropriate behavior.

Without evil, goodness would not be possible either.

Thus, the evil person who hurts us or others teaches us that we must be vigilant in choosing good, ethical and just behavior. It also affirms our commitment to teach our children how to be compassionate and caring individuals who love God and understand the consequences of our actions.

Sherry H. Blumberg
Assistant Professor of Jewish Education
Hebrew Union College-Jewish Institute of Religion
New York, New York

Why Are Bad People in the World?

In Hebrew there are two words for asking "why." One is *Madua*, and it seeks causes; the other is *Lamah*, and it looks for purposes. *Madua* looks to the past for explanations, causal relationships, historical background. *Lamah* looks to the future. It asks, why is X necessary, what valuable end or goal is served or met as a result of X existing?

Whether we ask *Madua* or *Lamah*, the problem of evil and of "bad people" is very difficult, and many of the wisest of people have studied this problem without discovering an answer that would satisfy everyone. The Jewish tradition has developed a great many such answers. It would appear that everyone who thinks about the problem comes up with an "answer" that, at best, "works" for him or her personally. Jews being a highly individualistic people, it is not surprising that there is no agreement on "the" answer to this problem. What follows is my own attempt to answer or cope with the problem personally.

Jews believe that people are born with the capacity for both good and bad. The basic building block of personality, what we call the *neshamah*, cannot be permanently stained. Therefore, *teshuvah*, turning away from evil and toward God, is always possible.

Madua —Causes

Some bad behavior is caused because human beings are sometimes born with terrible natural defects. A "crack baby" may be unable to respond to love except with violence. A child raised without love and support may not have a developed conscience. A person who lacks good food or adequate medical care or a safe home environment may be seriously handicapped in terms of understanding what it means to be good. People who are born healthy and are raised with loving, supportive parents in a wholesome environment can be expected, on the whole, to become normal and loving people. There may be an occasional exception, but studies of criminals reveal that criminal behavior is, more often than not, a result of serious deficits in the personal history of the criminal.

Yet people who are raised by good people also sometimes do bad things. This, I believe, happens because we are able to make choices. Sometimes we choose badly, selfishly, or thoughtlessly. We want something and we don't think about the long-term effects of that choice. Evil can result from those choices. Sometimes we may act purely on impulse—like animals—and that can lead to terrible forms of behavior. If people were programmed like computers and couldn't make choices, there might not be any bad people. But then there would not be any truly human beings either. To be human is to be free and to make choices. That is the essence of being human; it is also the source of tragedy.

Lamah —Purposes

I would say that all attempts to explain the "value" of evil are more or less unsatisfactory. There is an element of mystery in evil. All of our explanations fall short of the goal. We cannot explain the "value" of evil people. Yet we must react to them and their behavior, try to help them, while minimizing the damage that they do to themselves and to others.

I don't believe that God wants people to be bad. But God does want people to be people. I believe that with God's help, we can go a long way toward solving this problem. Our world would be a much better place for people if we concentrated on seeing to it that every baby that is born and every child that is raised *has* what he or she *needs* in order to become a good person. We can also teach people to think more clearly, to use their minds, to weigh the consequences of their actions, and we can give them opportunities to help each other and to feel the unique satisfaction that comes from being good people. That is part of what makes Jewish education so important for all of us.

On one level, there is no such thing as a bad person. Jews believe that people are born with the capacity for both good and bad. The basic building block of personality, what we call the *neshamah*, cannot be permanently stained. Therefore, *teshuvah*, turning away from evil and toward God, is always possible. In history, we have seen individuals like Adolph Hitler who have done such terrible things that they have come to be evil people. Yet, as a Jew, I believe that no one is permanently incapable of change. Someday we will know how to help those whom we cannot help today to change themselves. When that happens, there will be no evil people, only human beings who make mistakes but also learn to do good.

That is the message of Rosh Hashanah and Yom Kippur.

Saul Wachs, Professor of Jewish Education
Gratz College
Philadelphia, Pennsylvania

Why Do I Sometimes Do Bad Things?

Gaining im-pulse control and learning to use good judgment are acquired skills that you help your child develop through explora-tion and dialogue. By this process, you are showing your child that you want to help him in his ongo-ing struggle to choose good over evil, to under-stand right from wrong, and dan-gerous actions from harmless ones.

A child who phrases a question in this manner seems to already have a belief in his own badness, a belief that indicates a sense of low self-worth and shamefulness. It is important that parents and teachers respond in a way that does not encourage more self-criticism but instead offers insight and understanding. You might begin by telling your child that he himself is not bad, that he is not filled with badness. Then you can help him understand that doing bad things really means acting in ways that could be hurtful to himself or to others. Hitting another child, for example, is dangerous because it causes another child pain, just as running into a busy intersection could lead to an accident.

A child who asks why he is acting impulsively or dangerously is one who is already self-aware enough to know that behind every action is a feeling which is causing the behavior. Your help is needed for your child to discover the reasons for his actions. Perhaps he wanted to test his autonomy by trying something you've asked him not to do; or maybe he was angry about something else and displaced this emotion in a seemingly unrelated behavior. By asking questions, and offering to help uncover the underlying feelings, you can help your child develop the capacity to express his thoughts and feelings.

Judaism teaches us that we are not born evil, but rather are born with the capacity to choose good over evil. Gaining impulse control and learning to use good judgment are acquired skills that you help your child develop through exploration and dialogue. By this process, you are showing your child that you want to help him in his ongoing struggle to choose good over evil, to understand right from wrong, and dangerous actions from harmless ones.

Go a step further by encouraging your child to verbalize to you the things he'd like to do, even before he goes ahead and does them. Help him reason out for himself if these are wishes he should give in to. For example, your child may say he'd like to steal a candy bar from a well-stocked store. If, beforehand, you have given him permission to tell you of these kinds of wishes, then you can help him acknowledge and accept the reasons not to give in to this impulse. Provided you can listen without being critical, your child will feel accepted for all his thoughts and feelings, and learn the benefit of expressing himself rather than acting impulsively.

Karen B. Walant, Adjunct Professor
School of Social Work
New York University
New York, New York

Why Do I Sometimes Do Bad Things?

It is important to understand that Judaism is a very positive faith system. Our sacred literature is generally not negative or threatening. It is not the fear of punishment that motivates us to work to cultivate our good inclination as much as it is the simple reward of knowing we have done what is right.

Before directly answering the question, it would be good to define "bad things." What is bad for you may be good for me.

Generally, I suppose, when we deliberately or carelessly hurt another person we are doing something "bad." When we are endangering ourselves or others, like driving a car under the influence of alcohol or other drugs, or when we diminish ourselves or an institution, like our school, by cheating on a chemistry exam, we could safely say we are doing something bad.

What causes us to do these things? The Jewish tradition teaches that each of us has a *yetzer tov* and a *yetzer hara*, a "good inclination" and an "evil inclination." The role of religion, or of any other personal value system, is to help guide us along a more positive path. Occasionally we fail to overcome our negative or evil impulses, and in giving in to them we may do "bad things."

It is important to understand that Judaism is a very positive faith system. Our sacred literature is generally not negative or threatening. It is not the fear of punishment that motivates us to work to cultivate our good inclination as much as it is the simple reward of knowing we have done what is right.

Being human beings, we know that we are not always going to be good. Judaism emphasizes our sincere attempt to do what is right rather than our occasional failure. For we are human, and occasionally we will fail and commit a "sin," or in Hebrew a *chait*.

More than anything, the Jewish approach to life is one of growth and change. No behavior is absolute, nor is an individual ever completely incorrigible. If we do something bad, we are not destined to repeat that offense over and over again. We can evolve into more caring, sensitive and compassionate human beings by simply ceasing to do evil, and changing our behavior.

That progression, that human potential to grow and to change, is one of the reasons the Jewish religion exists. The ritual accouterments of Judaism certainly add color and meaning to our lives, but their primary function is to inspire us to eschew evil and to do good. The rest is commentary.

Robert S. Goldstein, Rabbi
Temple Emanuel
Andover, Massachusetts

CHAPTER V

Family, Friends and Future

1. Why is it important to have good family and friends?

2. Why do I get in fights with my brother and sister when I know I really love them?

3. If my parents get divorced, is it my fault?

4. When will I lose my parents?

5. Why do people make fun of other people?

6. Why do some people kill themselves?

7. What will I be when I grow up?

The preceding sections illustrate that Jewish wisdom has much to teach us about God and holiness, life and death, good and evil. In this section, we will see that Jewish tradition has much to teach us about day-to-day living with ourselves and with others. In fact, there may be no other religious tradition which has been so devoted to the matters of life in this world, as opposed to the matters of life in the world-to-come. Perhaps it is a very good thing that this is the case; judging from the contents of this section, it is clear that our children have many questions about growing up in this world.

They have asked, for instance, "What will I be when I grow up?" This is a question seemingly every child asks. It is a question we ourselves wondered about once upon a time. Try as we might to make our children's lives simple and idyllic, the normal process of growth and maturation introduces complexity and conflict into their childhoods. With the passing of years, our children become individuals who see themselves as distinct from their parents, their siblings, and their peers.

Despite the developing independence of our children, they really wish reassurance and nurturing when it comes to questions about their appearance, their worth, their abilities, and the security of their lives and the lives of those who are most important to them. Perhaps the one piece of advice most experts would offer in response to our children's questions is to assure them that they matter to us, that they are loved, and that they will be cared for.

From the kinds of questions our children have asked in this section, it seems clear that growing up in families and in the world-at-large help them learn about life with people. Even at very young ages, our children sense the pain and unhappiness of others just as they sense their joy. Children know when there is trouble in the family. They know when a parent is sad. They know when a peer has been hurt by the teasing of other peers.

Family and peer group are the two most important worlds in which our children grow up. Anything which threatens the well-being of any member of these groups threatens our children and their inner security. While illness, marital strife, sibling rivalry, and peer conflict do occur, we are advised to be honest, candid, patient, and reassuring in our responses to our children.

Why Is It Important to Have Good Family and Friends?

The most important people in our lives are our families. From our families we receive food, shelter and clothing, as well as the intangible things of life—love and security, identity and self-esteem, values.

Our parents are partners with God in creating, nurturing and guiding us. While their genes are our *material* building blocks, their values and the way they live their lives are our *moral and spiritual* building blocks.

Brothers and sisters are important too. A friend may be a friend for quite some time, but a sister or a brother is for life. Grandparents and other relatives give us an added sense of family security and identity. Through time spent together and stories told, they contribute to our understanding of what is special about our family and about ourselves.

Good friends are also important. As it says in the Ethics of the Fathers, "there is nothing better than a good friend, nothing worse than a bad friend" (2:13).

All of us want to have friends our own age. A true friend is someone who accepts us as we are and does not try to change us. That is important because each one of us has to find out what makes us special. If we are always trying to impress others by imitating someone else, we will never find what is special and unique about ourselves.

Still, friends have a big influence on us. Although each of us is different and each of us is an individual, most of us at some time will have friends we want to emulate. Maimonides recommends that we should only have friends who are good people. If we do, then we will be influenced for good. But if our friends are dishonest and like to do things that hurt others or are destructive, we may sometimes be tempted to go along with them.

The most important people in our lives are our families. From our families we receive food, shelter and clothing, as well as the intangible things of life—love and security, identity and self-esteem, values.

Of course, friends must be earned. If we want to have a good friend, we must *be* a good friend. This requires sensitivity, honesty, and caring.

Donald B. Rosoff, Rabbi
Temple B'nai Or
Morristown, New Jersey

Why Is It Important to Have Good Family and Friends?

Every person is a member of a family. When we are part of a family we feel safe, loved, and cared for. We may have our differences on occasion. We may argue once in a while and even think that sometimes we want to be part of a different family. Yet when we really begin to think about it, we realize that we would not trade our own family for another, no matter what. In a family we can be whoever we want to be because of the love, mutual trust, and respect we all have for each other. The family unit provides a safe environment to share feelings, ideas, thoughts, and fears.

So too with friends. Good friends, like family, allow us to be ourselves. Friendship is also based on love, trust and respect. Good friends may sometimes get angry with each other or say things that hurt; but most of the time good friends are there when we need them. Just like a mom and dad, brothers and sisters, they love us unconditionally and accept us for who we are.

Our tradition teaches us that a good family and good friends are like treasures. When we have a treasure we care for it, protect it, and treat it with pride. We feel special because we have the treasure. When we are lucky enough to have a good family and good friends, we too become precious, a part of the treasure.

Our tradition teaches us that a good family and good friends are like treasures. When we have a treasure we care for it, protect it, and treat it with pride. We feel special because we have the treasure. When we are lucky enough to have a good family and good friends, we too become precious, a part of the treasure.

Janice Alper, Family Education Specialist
Bureau of Jewish Education
Los Angeles, California

155

Why Is It Important to Have Good Family and Friends?

Most of the news tells about people who did not have good-enough family or friends. We are all skilled from birth at finding what we need in others—and turning away from what we do not need. That is why it's news when that does not happen.

Most of the news tells about people who did not have good-enough family or friends. We are all skilled from birth at finding what we need in others—and turning away from what we do not need. That is why it's news when that does not happen.

King Solomon was a good-enough friend when he solved the problem of which of two women claiming to be a baby's mother had the rightful claim. He said he would divide the baby in two—thereby moving the good-enough mother to renounce her claim in the interest of the baby's survival.

The king shared with the real mother a concern for raising children in a world full of surprises. As a separate person, he had the power to create a crisis which permitted the mother to reveal herself clearly. These are the important qualities of a friend: sharing our concerns, lending us power, helping us define ourselves.

The mother fought fiercely to stay connected to her baby, but she knew when she needed the king's help. And she could not forget for a moment that her child's interest came first. These are the important qualities of family: a fierce devotion to staying connected, seeking all the outside resources needed, resolving conflicts in the best interest of each individual's survival and growth.

The other woman—full of false and exclusive claims that would compel her child to grow up addicted to escape—this woman makes the headlines. But the good-enough family and friend create the good-enough world we live in.

And that world, that friend, that family need us just as much as we need them.

Don Shapiro, Psychologist
New York, New York

Why Do I Get in Fights with My Brother and Sister When I Know I Really Love Them?

Families are central to Jewish life. Our world revolves around traditions that are passed down from generation to generation, from parent to child. We learn a lot from family life. From our parents' behaviors we learn how adults have relationships, how men and women interact. We learn about honoring our own parents from the way in which our parents honor their parents, our grandparents.

We are taught to honor and cherish our parents. But where is it written that we should love or care about our brothers and sisters? Indeed, this is an implicit part of our cultural heritage which we learn from being a part of a family. We learn about caring about our brothers and sisters, in part, from the way our parents deal with our aunts and uncles, their brothers and sisters.

But how do we feel about our own brothers and sisters? Sometimes they make us so angry that we want to give up on them, to throw them out of our lives, to yell, "I've had it with this jerk! I can't take it anymore." At other times we are grateful to have someone to share our dreams, fears, and hopes with in a very special way. Beyond that, we know that if anything ever happened to our brother or sister, we would always be there for them—to help them through the tough times, to cheer them on—because we really do love them.

So why then do we fight with our siblings? When you get down to it, there is no way to avoid fighting with a sister or brother. It's bound to happen because we spend so much time together, and so many issues arise during the day, week, month, and year.

Sometimes sisters and brothers fight because they want their parents' attention, and one is jealous because the other one seems to be getting too much of the parents' time and energy. Jealousy may also come up if one sibling does

It is natural to get into fights with your brothers and sisters because everyday life brings problems along with it for people who live together. The challenge is to learn to work out the problems so that we will have this skill as a tool for the rest of our lives.

better, either academically or athletically, than the other one. Sometimes we think that the rules of the household are more fair for our siblings than for us. We see the same thing happen with friends and coworkers as we grow up. The way in which we learn to settle our problems with our brothers and sisters will help us to learn to have healthy relationships in our lives with our friends and coworkers.

The answer to this question, then, is that it is natural to get into fights with your brothers and sisters because life brings problems along with it for people who live together. The challenge is to learn to work out the problems so that we will have this skill as a tool for the rest of our lives.

Gail Teicher Fellus
Director of Curriculum Development
Department for Religious Education
Union of American Hebrew Congregations
New York, New York

Why Do I Get in Fights with My Brother and Sister When I Know I Really Love Them?

The child asking this question expresses great compassion, sensitivity, and concern as a very loving member of a family. This same child may be experiencing confusion and guilt over these opposing feelings of fighting and loving, which may be central to the motivation that brought up this question. This child must be helped to understand that fighting is a very normal growing and learning experience in living within a family—a process that helps us to develop skills necessary for life in the world outside of our own family.

The Jewish tradition has long grappled with the problem of sibling rivalry. The psalmist declares, "How good and how pleasant it is that brothers sit together" (Psalm 133:1). Yet this seems to be written with the understanding of how hard it is to achieve this ideal. The Bible dramatizes stories of sibling rivalry: Jacob steals the birthright from his older brother, Esau (Genesis 25:33); Rachel and Leah are envious of each other (Genesis 30); Joseph's brothers are jealous because he is their father's favorite (Genesis 37:1-4).

Though our sibling rivalries rarely reach biblical proportions, the tensions of family life reflect similar concerns. The makeup of family relationships involves the interaction of its members, parents and children, in good times and bad. When people who love each other live together day after day and are affected by different personalities as well as various external influences, it is a quite natural and frequent occurrence that annoyances, disagreements, or conflicts take place. Shared bedrooms and possessions, common interests, or competition for parental recognition often trigger these conflicts between siblings.

It is important to let the child know that in all of our lives there are situations that cause us to feel frustration, anger, or

The Jewish tradition has long grappled with the problem of sibling rivalry. The psalmist declares, "How good and how pleasant it is that brothers sit together" (Psalm 133:1). Yet this seems to be written with the understanding of how hard it is to achieve this ideal.

159

upset; and that it is normal and acceptable to have these feelings. It is also very healthy to express these feelings—to let them out. Of course, we must guide the child by giving him or her the tools to express these negative feelings verbally rather than physically, emphasizing communication, sharing, cooperation, and compromise as means to resolution. Help the child learn to separate his or her feelings so that the anger is directed toward the situation that has gotten in the way, rather than toward his brother or sister. It is difficult to have feelings of love for someone at the same time that you are provoked enough to fight. Let the child know that feelings of anger and fights are short-lived, but feelings of love shared by siblings seem to endure.

We should always feel safe in being able to express our feelings within our own family, still knowing that sometimes we cannot do so in other situations. Families provide us with unconditional love; the knowledge that we will be loved by the other members of our family no matter what happens—even when we fight. Since today's children seem to grow up so fast, and are burdened with so many responsibilities, it is important to allow them to feel and act like children—to let them know that it is natural for brothers and sisters to fight, and that they should not worry about misplaced feelings of love.

Children must be guided by their parents to learn to work out their feelings toward negative situations involving their brothers and sisters, along with the reassurance of unconditional love. Learning how to resolve sibling conflicts helps us to develop skills for building healthy relationships throughout our adult lives.

Ronni S. Mandell, Educator
Jewish Family Congregation
South Salem, New York

If My Parents Get Divorced, Is It My Fault?

The belief of children that they are somehow responsible for their parents' divorce is an all-too-common occurrence. While children of all ages may harbor these sentiments, such feelings are especially prevalent among younger children, who are prone to equate their own secret wishes or fears with external realities. As a result, when parents inform a child that they are divorcing, fact and fantasy tend to become confused.

For example, anger at a parent's scolding may have caused the child to openly or privately express the desire that the parent leave the home. Or, in the heat of an altercation, parents may have verbalized their frustrations over a child's behavior by exclaiming, "We don't know what to do with you, you are upsetting everyone in the family!"

Generally, in the normal course of family interaction, these incidents are soon forgotten. However, during a divorce, children may remember these events and conclude that they have somehow caused the marriage to come apart. Their anxieties are now compounded by the terror of their own seeming omnipotence and remorse over what they have done.

It is therefore essential that parents make it explicitly clear to their children, whatever their ages, that the divorce had nothing to do with them, that they are loved and will be cared for despite the end of the marriage. These assurances may have to be repeated on any number of occasions. Parents should not wait for children to mention any incriminating thoughts before reiterating their love. Prospects that children will do so voluntarily are unlikely.

If at some point in the past the child stated that the parents ought to divorce, the incident should now be deliberately recalled. Parents should remind the child of what happened

> **It is essential that parents make it explicitly clear to their children, whatever their ages, that the divorce had nothing to do with them, that they are loved and will be cared for despite the end of the marriage.**

161

and stress that there is no connection whatsoever between the child's statement and the actual divorce. Children need to be told that in the heat of an argument we all lose our tempers and say things we do not mean.

A familiar by-product of divorce is a reduction in the family's standard of living. The old adage that two families cannot live as cheaply as one is an all-too-tangible fact of separation. It may be necessary to move from the family residence, leaving friends and possibly changing schools. Any lingering sense of liability can only add to a child's distress over these impending dislocations. The matter should again be addressed firmly but lovingly.

Although children in some instances will not assume that they are at fault, and in others will persist in denying the idea, the possibility should not be ignored. Parents should address it jointly and individually. The conviction that they are blameless can go a long way toward helping children cope with the unavoidable anguish and readjustment attendant to the breakup of a marriage.

Sanford Seltzer, Director of Research
Union of American Hebrew Congregations
Boston, Massachusetts

162

If My Parents Get Divorced, Is It My Fault?

When parents get divorced it is not the child's fault. Though it may be normal for a child to feel guilty about his or her parents' separation, it is important to help the child understand that he or she cannot control the feelings his or her parents have toward one another. With any divorce there are two issues children have to deal with. The first is to understand the changed nature of the relationship that now exists between the mother and the father. The second is to understand how important and special the relationship is that will always exist between parent and child.

Jewish tradition views the union of two people as something sacred. Little is more sacred than the way two people relate to one another. When two people are in love, marry, and create a family, it is with the sincere hope that their relationship will last. Sometimes, for many reasons, relationships don't work out as planned. The rabbis, in their wisdom, understood this. Acknowledging both the sanctity of marriage and the sanctity of the individual's right to live a fulfilling life, they created a system which allows for couples to get divorced.

To be in a loving and caring relationship with someone is special. Clearly something so special should not be lessened by having people who no longer feel that special way toward each other be forced to stay together.

The unique and special relationship between parents and their children need not be diminished by a divorce. Perhaps the best piece of advice I ever received when my parents got divorced was when someone told me that of all the relationships one will have in one's lifetime, the only two people that one will always have a relationship with, the only two people in the world that one can never *not* have a relationship with, are a mother and father. Knowing this, it is up to

With any divorce there are two issues children have to deal with. The first is to understand the changed nature of the relationship that now exists between the mother and the father. The second is to understand how important and special the relationship is that will always exist between parent and child.

each individual to try and make that relationship as good as possible.

Though parents may no longer choose to live together, to the children involved, these two people will always be mom and dad. As hard as it may be, now is the time to "turn the hearts of the children to the parents and the hearts of the parents to the children" (Malachi 3:24).

Barnett J. Brickner, Assistant Rabbi
United Hebrew Congregation
St. Louis, Missouri

When Will I Lose My Parents?

Prepare for this question, which surely will be asked, by learning to analyze the question itself.

Engage the child in a conversation that will reveal the motivation for the question. Did a friend's parent die? Did the child read something about a death? Is a parent ill? Or does the question simply show a slowly growing awareness of the reality of death? Knowing the child's concern will help you craft the best response.

Note also the language the child uses. The words "die" and "death" do not appear in the question above; only the euphemistic word "lose" appears. The adult needs to speak directly of death and dying in order to teach the child that these are natural parts of life. Death ought not to be conceived of as something bad, but as a sad yet acceptable part of life. In answering the question honestly but reassuringly, you will respond to the child's unspoken need for a sense of stability and security in the world.

The answer itself might be: "Not for a long time. Not until you are big and strong and grown up. But once in a very long while, a mommy or daddy dies before their child is grown up. When that happens, someone else who is big and strong and full of love will take care of the boy or girl. It's very sad when that happens, but it's all right. And it's hardly likely at all that it could happen to you and your mom or dad."

Use examples the child can understand. I have often used a series of comic strips from Bill Watterson's "Calvin and Hobbes," where the boy sees a raccoon die and wrestles with these kinds of questions. Speaking in the child's world can help the child as he or she also wrestles with the questions.

In answering the question, your own attitude will shine through clearly. So, before the child asks the question, think yourself about issues related to death and dying. A child will

Death ought not to be conceived of as something bad, but as a sad yet acceptable part of life. In answering the question honestly but reassuringly, you will respond to the child's unspoken need for a sense of stability and security in the world.

quickly feel your clarity and strength—or sense your anxiety and fear. If you feel a wave of panic at imagining answering the question, take your preparation a little farther. Spend some time now talking to someone about your own feelings. When the moment comes, the more you have dealt with these issues yourself, the more strength, calm, and sense of security you can communicate to the child.

Carole L. Meyers, Rabbi
Temple Sinai
Glendale, California

When Will I Lose My Parents?

Your parents are not going to die for a very long time, not until you are much older and married and have children of your own. You will never be left alone. If something does happen to your parents there are relatives and friends who will always be here to take care of you.

Though your parents will be with you for a very long time, one day they *will* die. Everyone dies. No living thing lives forever. Some things live longer than others. There are turtles that live for hundreds of years. Mosquitos live only for a few weeks. (I wonder how long an elephant lives?) People live to around seventy-five years old, and a few people live to one hundred. (Moses lived to be one hundred and twenty!) We can live for a long time, but we don't live forever.

Even when we are dead, we're not alone. The Torah tells us that in the beginning, when God first made people, God blew a breath into them. Since that time, there has been a *neshamah*, a little bit of God's breath, inside every person. It stays with us wherever we go and remains a part of us as we grow up. When we die, our *neshamah* goes back to God, together with the *neshamot* from all the people that have died.

Your parents will be with you for a long time to come, and God will always be with you, now and forever.

Jeffrey A. Marx, Rabbi
Santa Monica Synagogue
Santa Monica, California

The Torah tells us that in the beginning, when God first made people, God blew a breath into them. Since that time, there has been a *neshamah*, a little bit of God's breath, inside every person. It stays with us wherever we go and remains a part of us as we grow up. When we die, our *neshamah* goes back to God, together with the *neshamot* from all the people that have died.

167

Why Do People Make Fun of Other People?

Often insecure students feel the need to strengthen their own self-concept by picking on those whom they perceive as more vulnerable than they are. These students are jealous, insecure, and attempt to build themselves up at the expense of their classmates.

This question is one which we frequently receive from students who find themselves the object of peer cruelty. Often insecure students feel the need to strengthen their own self-concept by picking on those whom they perceive as more vulnerable than they are. These students are jealous, insecure, and attempt to build themselves up at the expense of their classmates.

In a time when we see major changes in the makeup of the Jewish family, when students come to our schools from a wide variety of family configurations, they look to the synagogue and the Jewish school for a sense of identity.

We can do a great deal with Judaic sources to help our students understand that our tradition teaches all of us to accept those who are different or have special needs and to provide for them.

For example, in Exodus 3:10, we learn that our great leader, Moses, had a speech impediment. "But Moses said to the Lord, 'Please, O Lord, I have never been a man of words, either in times past or now that You have spoken to Your servant: I am slow of speech and slow of tongue.' And the Lord said to him, 'Who gives man speech? Who makes him dumb or deaf, seeing or blind? Is it not I, the Lord?'" Yet Moses was chosen by God to be not only the leader of His people but His spokesperson to the people of the world.

The message is clear: we don't value people because of the unimportant things—e.g., how they look or how they dress—but because of their intrinsic value. Moses is chosen for his ability to lead, and the people of Israel do not question his leadership because of his speech impediment. This is a basic teaching of our Jewish heritage that we want to pass on to the next generation.

We can also point to the Holiness Code, Leviticus 19:1, which culminates with verse 18, "Love your neighbor as yourself." This verse, which has been called the "Golden Rule," demands for others the same kind of treatment we want for ourselves.

When children pick on one another or act in a cruel manner, we can point to this basic rule to help them focus on what they are doing and how they would feel if they were the target of being made fun of by other people.

Zena Sulkes, Educator
Congregaton Rodeph Shalom
Philadelphia, Pennsylvania

Why Do Some People Want to Kill Themselves?

Some people do not realize that bad situations pass and life circumstances will be better. Every now and then a person feels that it is too painful to continue living. Often, people think they can kill the part of them that is hurting, leaving the rest alive.

At some point in many people's lives they feel as if they want to kill themselves. It is not the thought that is disturbing, but the reality that some people actually follow through and either attempt or complete suicide.

Most suicidal feelings pass without being acted upon. The high value Jews place on living life makes it more difficult to explain why people would want to kill themselves. Most of the time, most people feel good about who they are and comfortable with themselves. However, there are times when life gets very hard and it hurts just to be alive. With patience, these times eventually pass, some more slowly than others, but everything becomes OK again. Usually people understand this. However, some people do not realize that bad situations pass and life circumstances will be better. Every now and then a person feels that it is too painful to continue living. Often, people think they can kill the part of them that is hurting, leaving the rest alive. They do not realize that death is a permanent solution to a passing problem. An individual in psychic pain—one who is very hurt or extremely angry, frequently finds it difficult to be rational. In their efforts to kill the hurt, people sometimes take drugs or drink alcoholic beverages. Substance abuse of this kind can bring death either directly or, by driving too fast or taking undue risks, indirectly.

Judaism teaches us that each life is very precious. Each person is special and unique. Personal value should be reinforced regularly. Life can be beautiful, but there are stressful times as well. As parents and teachers we must endeavor to teach our youth that they are significant and special, and that they should value their lives and the lives of all other people no matter what stresses they suffer.

Ellen Mack, Director of Education
Beth-El Congregation
Fort Worth, Texas

What Will I Be When I Grow Up?

To the child who asks, "What will I be when I grow up?" respond, "You will be all that you can be and all that I can help you be. You will be all that you want to be, and I promise to support you with all the help and love I can give."

Probably the most important element in responding to children's aspirations and anxieties concerning the future is to help them to understand that whatever they become will be good and right. There are no absolute rights and wrongs. Becoming is not a competition with anyone else. It is the fulfillment of self. It is who we have been, what we have done along the way. It is also who we can be because of lots of things about ourselves.

Everybody is always somebody. Everybody is always unique and important, depending how they look upon their accomplishments. As trite as it may sound, becoming the best at what it is you do, no matter what, is a full answer. This is, after all, the age of self-actualization.

What about the pressures that all youngsters feel as they look at mothers and fathers, aunts and uncles doing incredible things? What about the pressures they feel when they hear the adults express their envy at the position, power, or wealth of another? The expressed values of our society do not encourage youngsters to become what they really want to become, what they really feel inside, unless it contains the elements of power and wealth, prestige and fame. The American Jewish community is so overwhelming in its current position relative to the above that children feel inadequate. "How can I ever have what they have, become what they have become, do as well as they have done?" As difficult as it is to believe, they can become so much more. They can have a real sense of inner peace. They can know real *shalom*, real fullness of the spirit. How we respond as they become is the key. The message we convey about a life filled with nonmaterial values has got to be the way.

"I want to be a millionaire" just is not an appropriate aspiration for one who is really concerned about what he or she will be. One cannot be a millionaire. One can have a million dollars. It is unfortunate that the term has become a noun rather than just an adjective. One is a person of values who functions in a particular way within society, who does certain things in the course of daily life, to provide for self and others and to contribute to the community. That is what one will be.

To the child who asks, "What will I be when I grow up?" respond, "You will be all that you can be and all that I can help you be. You will be all that you want to be, and I promise to support you with all the help and love I can give."

Allan L. Smith, Director
Youth Division
Union of American Hebrew Congregations
New York, New York

What Will I Be When I Grow Up?

"In the world-to-come," Reb Zusya replied, "they will not ask me why I was not like Solomon, they will not ask me why was I not like Moses. In the world-to-come they will ask me: 'Zusya, why were you not like Zusya?'"

It is an old joke: The Jewish grandmother is walking on the boardwalk with her two precious grandsons when a neighbor approaches and pinches their cheeks. "Oh, such handsome boys," she says. "How old are they?" "Well," replies the grandmother, "the doctor is four, and the lawyer is six!"

There seems to be a lot of pressure on Jewish young people these days: pressure to do well in school, pressure to go to the best colleges and graduate schools, pressure to become successful and professional.

To be sure, medicine and law are, from a Jewish perspective, both respected and praiseworthy career choices. Maimonides, the great rabbinic scholar, was also an eminent physician in his day. The rabbis themselves were not only spiritual leaders but legal decisors.

What is perhaps less well known, however, is that before the destruction of the Second Temple in Jerusalem, most Jews, or Israelites, were actually farmers. Indeed Judaism as a religion is heavily influenced by its agricultural roots.

Throughout the centuries Jews have participated in commerce and trade; they have made contributions in the fields of art and science and sports and literature; they have served as soldiers and politicians, statesmen and stateswomen. There have even been Jewish prime ministers!

So what are you going to be when you grow up? Whatever you want to be? Well, almost. There is also the matter of hard work, desire, dedication, and sometimes a little luck to be considered.

What is clear in Judaism is that your career decisions must be based on your own talents, interests, and inclinations. No one else, not even the most trusted, beloved, or well-intentioned advisor, will have to live your life for you.

The career which you choose will most likely encompass half of your waking hours. You had better enjoy what you are doing and find satisfaction in it if you hope to find satisfaction in life.

Certainly the earning of a living is a legitimate consideration in choosing a career, but it should not be the overriding motivation. Be true to your own feelings; set your own goals.

Before he died, it is said, Reb Zusya was trembling with fear. His disciples were puzzled. "Reb Zusya," they asked, "why are you trembling? You have lived your life with the wisdom of Solomon and the uprightness of Moses. What do you have to fear? In the world-to-come you will certainly be rewarded."

"In the world-to-come," Reb Zusya replied, "they will not ask me why I was not like Solomon, they will not ask me why was I not like Moses. In the world-to-come they will ask me: 'Zusya, why were you not like Zusya?'"

It is therefore our fervent hope that when you grow up you will be uniquely, independently, quintessentially . . . you.

Paul M. Yedwab, Assistant Rabbi
Temple Israel
West Bloomfield, Michigan

What Will I Be When I Grow Up?

Parents can't dictate what you should do; hopefully, they will inspire you to find a life's path that fulfills your unique talents.

The first thing you have to realize is that when you grow up you will be still be yourself—just more fully realized. The things you feel and experience now, even when they don't make sense or when they downright confuse or sadden you, all make up the developing raw materials that will fulfill your adult being. Growth, sometimes painful, sometimes bewildering, is nevertheless the only road to a deeper understanding of what we were born into: human life.

Don't be too certain about what career choice you will ultimately make. The world is changing very quickly; there has been more information transmitted since you were born than in all of previous history! Don't be so hard on yourself when you feel you can't make up your mind about what you will be. Remember that inside of you there lives a heart that needs time, gentleness, and patience in order to learn itself. The *people* you meet will affect you and guide you to decisions. The world is changing, but the need for calm and deliberate growing and knowing will never change.

Your parents can be role models for your career decisions, but they do not dictate your choice. Perhaps more important than *what* your parents do is whether or not they're *happy* doing it. It's more important that your profession gives you creative satisfaction than if it's what your mom or dad did. If you fail at something, that will only prove that you are a human being. If you push them gently, your parents will probably admit that they failed at one thing or another along the way. Parents can't dictate what you should do; hopefully, they will inspire you to find a life's path that fulfills your unique talents.

Ben Kamin, Rabbi
The Temple - Tifereth Israel
Cleveland, Ohio

CHAPTER VI

The Best of the Rest

1. Why do I have to go to Hebrew school?

2. Why should I go to synagogue?

3. Why do we have holidays?

4. If you are Jewish, do you have to follow the rules?

5. Why do we have Jewish rituals?

6. Is it important to wear a yarmulke and tallit at services?

7. What is so important about Bar/Bat Mitzvah?

8. Why don't Jewish people celebrate Christmas?

This last section deals with rites, rituals, and sacred celebrations. Although most of us, including our children, do not think about it too much, we live in a world replete with rites, rituals, and sacred celebrations. Our ballgames begin with the National Anthem, the sacred hymn of our country. Many school days begin with the "watchwords" of our nation's civil faith, the Pledge of Allegiance. And don't we all march in the parades of sacred occasions on our civil calendar like Memorial Day?

Rites and rituals help our children integrate the most fundamental values we hold. Actually, they are multisensory learning strategies which provide visual, olfactory, auditory, oral, and kinesthetic means for our children to see, smell, hear, taste, and feel the basic ordering principles of our sacred and secular worlds.

Sacred ceremonies like holiday celebrations and life cycle events make ordinary moments in life extraordinary. They provide a structure within which we can explore the transcendent dimensions of life. Their observance responds to many of the important questions life raises. They enable us to mark time more consciously and infuse that time with lessons and value. Just as secular holidays teach our children about the American heritage, Jewish holidays teach children about their Jewish heritage. The Passover Seder retells the Exodus from Egyptian slavery, but it also does much more than that. It gives our children a sense of belonging to others who share their heritage. It teaches them Jewish lessons about oppression, about idolatry, about the presence of the Divine in their lives, and about hope.

Children feel comfortable with rites, rituals, and celebrations when they are familiar with them and with the people with whom they will observe them. On the other hand, when they are invited to participate in a ritual which is unfamiliar, or celebrate a holiday they don't know, or wear a piece of sacred attire which is strange to them, our children are bound to ask us the kinds of questions contained in this section. Sometimes these questions seek information to explain the unfamiliar. Sometimes these questions challenge us parents to explain our reasons for requesting our children's participation in rituals and ceremonies which we do not observe ourselves. For example, we might be asked "Why should I go to synagogue?" when we ourselves don't go, or "What is so important about Bar and Bat Mitzvah?" when we ourselves don't show any interest in Jewish study.

Finally, questions about observance obviate the differences among the various denominations of Judaism quite sharply. Whereas Reform Jews hold that each individual must decide for himself which traditions to observe, halachic

Jews believe that all of the traditions which are prescribed by the Written Law (the Torah), the Oral Law (the teachings of the classical sages), and interpreted by the great rabbis of the succeeding ages are applicable today and must be observed. The experts whose advice was sought in response to our children's questions represent many of the different positions along the spectrum of Jewish ritual observance from more liberal to more orthodox. One of the reasons that at least two responses were invited to these questions is to give you the opportunity to make your own choices.

Why Do I Have to Go to Hebrew School?

The perennial question. Every child asks it at least once—and probably twice a week. Answers vary. Perhaps the most important reason for Jewish schools—and for you to send your child to them—is to provide your child with a direct, guided interaction with Judaism. By providing a sacred context, Jewish schools help the child reach closer to God. Jewish education is a means to an end, not an end in itself. It cannot replace the nurturance and loving support that only a family can provide. Nor should it attempt to do so. Yet it strives to help equip the Jewish child with the skills and resources necessary to function responsibly in the contemporary Jewish community.

But to fully and honestly answer your child's question, you yourself have to feel the answer and believe it. A wishy-washy answer will not suffice. If it is not deeply compelling, your child won't believe it, and—if the truth be told—neither will you. Probe deeply inside yourself. What is the basic motivation that moves you to send your child to a Jewish school? Do you want to provide your child with a sense of heritage or Jewish roots? Do you want your child to make up for your own lack of Jewish knowledge? Are you responding to the wishes of grandparents? Do you want your child to become a *mentsch*? All of these possibilities are indispensable ingredients and the beginning of great answers. But there is more. The Jewish future depends on it—and so does the entire world. Without the survival of the educated Jew, Judaism will not survive. Without the survival of Judaism, the world will not survive. Think about it. Then go drive carpool.

Kerry M. Olitzky, Director
School of Education
Hebrew Union College-Jewish Institute of Religion
New York, New York

Why Should I Go to Synagogue?

The question presupposes a reluctance on the part of the young person to go to synagogue—no such question would be asked about ice cream parlors or movie theaters! My response, on the other hand, presupposes a synagogue life that is engaging, relevant, and empowering to congregants young and old. If your synagogue falls short of this ideal, help improve it! Encourage your children to do the same. Modern Judaism is a dance, not a military march. It needs the energy, the creativity—even the inspiriting naivete—of those, like our youngsters, who thirst for the ideal in their spiritual lives.

Ideally, then, the synagogue is to Judaism what the home is to the family: a hallowed place of genuine intimacy, of respite from the turmoil of daily living, of healthful habits or disciplines, and of dialogue that can strengthen us as we move out into the world. Like the home, the synagogue is a place of *mutual obligation* and *interdependency*; our presence is appreciated, our absence is felt, especially in times of sorrow or *simcha*.

The synagogue stands at the crossroads of ancient tradition and contemporary community; there is no other institution, neither museum nor clubhouse, that so dynamically blends the process of remembrance and recreation. Jewish memory thus becomes a memory of the mind *and* heart; our learning and our yearnings combine into an identity that will continue to grow throughout our lives. It is by this process of foundation-building, and none other, that the Jewish people learn to be Jews and achieve their collective continuity in each generation.

The synagogue is also a place, unique in our secular society, where young Jews can concentrate upon their spiritual concerns without embarrassment. They can ask

The synagogue provides a unique opportunity to experience a community in which the quest for God is the great equalizer: competitiveness, the generation gap, and other forces of divisiveness among people are rendered irrelevant by the binding force of Judaism.

questions about belief in God, the meaning of life and death, the role of evil in the world, and they will find not only that their questions are taken seriously, but that they are participants in a tradition that is passionate about such questions. The very environment of the synagogue, in which the quest for holiness is central, can yield that sense of holiness; it requires only the surrender of shyness, apathy, laziness, embarrassment, or other forms of resistance. Prayers are thus answered by the simple act of praying; as one talmudic master taught, "he who rises from his prayer a better Jew, a better human being, his prayer has been answered."

Answers and certainties they may not find, and this may frustrate the childhood concern for sure-footedness, for the sense of confidence that certainties may render. Instead, the synagogue breeds *maturity*: the recognition and acceptance of complexity, and a commitment to grapple with that complexity. Judaism provides the tools; ours is a religious tradition that closely scans the fabric of daily life to find the holy threads that run throughout.

Finally, the synagogue provides the fellowship of Jews— all shapes, all sizes, all ages. The synagogue provides a unique opportunity to experience a community in which the quest for God is the great equalizer: competitiveness, the generation gap, and other forces of divisiveness among people are rendered irrelevant by the binding force of Judaism.

Alexander M. Schindler, President
Union of American Hebrew Congregations
New York, New York

Why Do We Have Holidays?

One hour is not just like another. There are hours for work and hours for play. There is a time for planting and a time for harvesting. We divide time into different types of days and seasons according to our use of time.

When we reach out toward God and toward all that is of eternal value, we realize that time can be either ordinary or holy. We spend ordinary time in the pursuit of our daily needs. We spend holy time—holidays—seeking and acting out the highest goals of life. Holy time connects us to God, to our community, to our history, and to the highest within ourselves.

The Torah teaches that God has favored us with certain holidays. God commands us to observe Shabbat so that we may become holy through rest, worship, and study. God gives us the festivals of Sukkot, Pesach, and Shavuot to give thanks, to remember our origin, and to worship God as Creator, as Savior, and as Giver of the Torah. God gives us the High Holy Days as a time to return to goodness and to seek forgiveness. We Jews have created additional holidays to remember important moments in our history.

Our goal as Jews is to make all time holy. We describe the perfect future for which we yearn as "the time that is all Shabbat"—the time when every day is a holy day.

Stephen Wylen, Rabbi
Temple Hesed
Scranton, Pennsylvania

We spend holy time—holidays—seeking and acting out the highest goals of life. Holy time connects us to God, to our community, to our history, and to the highest within ourselves.

Why Do We Have Holidays?

This question may arise from simple curiosity, or it may be a challenge because the child objects to participating in a holiday celebration. The goal is to help the child understand that when we celebrate Jewish holidays, we remember important events in our past, we feel part of the Jewish people, and we affirm those values that are important to us today. Along with the actual answer to the question, it is important to affirm the value of the child and his or her question.

There are two approaches: first, a direct narrative answer; second, develop an answer that is developed through a series of questions posed to the child. Both approaches begin with the child's experience with holidays and move toward a more general answer which applies to all holidays.

Using the first approach, you can ask the child to tell you her favorite holiday. Then, simply recall with her what happened, why it happened, and what it means today. Finally, you can generalize from this specific instance and indicate that we have holidays because in celebrating an event in the past, we enrich our lives now by learning important lessons, making us feel close to the Jewish people, to family and friends, and to God. For example, "On Passover we had a Seder where we remembered the Exodus of our people, the Jewish people, from Egypt. We brought our family together, felt connected to the Jewish people, and expressed the hope that those who are now enslaved will soon be free."

Using the second approach, ask the child some of these questions: "Let's answer your question by looking at one of the holidays you have celebrated. Choose a holiday you enjoyed; for example, Hanukkah, Passover, Thanksgiving, or even your birthday. What did you enjoy about it? What

184

happened? What was the holiday about? Why did people come together? Since the event happened so long ago, what does it have to do with us?" Here the child may have some trouble, so you may want to help with the answer, make it a rhetorical question that you answer, or simply not ask the question and go on to explain the relevance.

You can then generalize from this discussion and say, "We have holidays because there are events in the past, such as Hanukkah (Passover, Thanksgiving, your birthday), which we want to remember now. For example, in celebrating Hanukkah we remember the dedication of Jews to Judaism in the past, and that encourages us to protect our people and our faith today."

Adam Fisher, Rabbi
Temple Isaiah
Stony Brook, New York

If You Are Jewish Do You Have to Follow All the Rules?

In Judaism what you do is even more important than what you believe. In this way Judaism is a very different kind of religion from Christianity. Some people say that Judaism is a religion of deed and not of creed. So what we do is very important.

This is one of the most important questions a Jew can ask. In Judaism what you do is even more important than what you believe. In this way Judaism is a very different kind of religion from Christianity. Some people say that Judaism is a religion of deed and not of creed. So what we do is very important.

The things that Jews do are called mitzvot. Some people translate this term as "law." A better English equivalent is "commandment." Best of all is just to use the Hebrew term. According to Jewish tradition, there are six hundred and thirteen mitzvot in the Torah. These mitzvot may be ritual or ethical, time-bound or constant, directed to one particular historical moment or binding for all times.

We Jews feel called on to fulfill the mitzvot, not out of fear, but out of love. The mitzvot are a way we show our devotion to God. God gave us the mitzvot as a symbol of the covenant, the special relationship that exists between God and the Jewish people. The mitzvot are the hallmark of Jewish life. They show that we know we live our lives in the presence of God. We remind ourselves of this idea in every service when we connect the idea of love of God with the performance of mitzvot. In every Jewish service we pray the V'ahavta, which says:

You shall love the Lord your God with all your heart and soul and might. Set these words, which I command you this day, upon your heart. . . . That you may *remember and do* all My mitzvot, and be holy unto your God.

When we pray the *V'ahavta* we hear the idea "that you may remember and do *all* my mitzvot." This raises an important question. Do we have to do all the mitzvot to be good Jews? If we do not do them all, does that mean we are

186

not really Jewish? Is it possible to do only some of them and still love God?

Sometimes we imagine that earlier generations of Jews were good Jews in a way that we are not—they did all of the mitzvot, even when we tend only to do some. Yet it turns out that we are not the first generation of Jews to wonder about whether we should do all of the mitzvot. Earlier generations understood that some of the six hundred and thirteen mitzvot could not be performed at all. Some of them were given specifically for the time when the Temple was in existence—mitzvot of sacrifice, celebration and observance in the Temple itself. These mitzvot could not be performed after the Temple was destroyed. Today for those Jews who believe and hope that the Temple will be rebuilt, these mitzvot can be studied now in the expectation and yearning that they will be called upon to rejuvenate them when the Temple is rebuilt.

Of the remaining mitzvot, Jews of earlier generations and all Jews today—even the most pious and rigorous—recognize that none of us can do all of them. Some are intended only for women—men cannot fulfill these mitzvot. Some are directed to men. Still others are directed to people at particular stages or circumstances in their lives. People not in those stages or circumstances are not called on, or able, to observe these mitzvot. For instance the laws of mourning do not apply to us when we are not mourners. One mitzvah calls on us to say a particular blessing when we are in the presence of a king. Most of us are never in a position to fulfill that mitzvah.

In the Talmud we read:

Rabbi Simlai taught: Six hundred and thirteen commandments were given to Moses. Then David reduced them to eleven in Psalm 15, beginning: "He who follows integrity, who does what is required and speaks the truth in his heart."

Micah reduced them to three:"Act justly, love mercy, and walk humbly with your God" (Micah 6:8).

Then came Isaiah and reduced them to two: "Keep justice and act with integrity" (Isaiah 56:1).

Amos reduced them to one: "Seek Me and live" (Amos 5:40).

Habakkuk also contained them in one: "But the righteous shall live by his faith" (Habakuk 2:4).

Akiva taught: "The great principle of the Torah is expressed in the commandment: 'Love your neighbor as you love yourself; I am the Lord' (Leviticus 19:18)."

In our day this is the question that divides Orthodox and Liberal Jews. The underlying ideology of Orthodoxy asserts that the more mitzvot you observe, the better Jew you are. Liberal Judaism has a different answer to this question. It does not follow that God or Jewish tradition demand that we do all the mitzvot or should feel ourselves drawn to do them all. Rather we should see the whole panoply of mitzvot as a kind of smorgasbord. A Jew should learn about all of the mitzvot and regard all of them as options for our personal life.

Reform Judaism tends to see a distinction between mitzvot that are moral or ethical and those that are ritual. Reform Jews see the mitzvot of moral and ethical life as binding and incumbent on all of us all the time. The other mitzvot—the ritual mitzvot—are options open to all of us. We "try on" these mitzvot. We are called on to explore them, to see if they fit us. Some become "our mitzvot," and these are the mitzvot that we have to do.

It sounds like there is a great gap between Orthodox and Liberal Jews. And in some ways there is. But in certain ways Orthodox and Liberal Jews *share* some important understandings. Both groups see that mitzvot are part of the lifeline that binds us to God and the Jewish people. They are the expression of what connects us to our history. The mitzvot connect us to other Jews, wherever they live and whatever the circumstances of their lives. Whether we feel called on to do them all or to choose from them, the act of engaging with mitzvot binds us to one another.

Our engagement with mitzvot grows out of our special relationship with God and our certainty that God cares about us. The doing of mitzvot is an expression of our love for God.

Daniel Polish, Rabbi
Temple Beth El
Birmingham, Michigan

If You Are Jewish Do You Have to Follow All the Rules?

Some Jews see Judaism as a religion of ethical, moral, and social rules that tell us how to be better people, drawing closer to all the peoples of the universe. Other Jews see Judaism as a series of rules laid down by God for the Jewish people to survive, grow strong, and protect themselves as a particular, special people.

What are the rules? At one level, for Jews there are rules in the Ten Commandments, the Torah, the Bible, the Mishnah, the Midrash, the Talmud, and the codes of Jewish law. There are many rules, and some are contradictory. The Torah tells us to love our neighbor as ourselves but also to wipe out certain neighboring peoples. Some Jews overlook one or the other of these rules. Some say that the harsh second rule is no longer valid, while others say that "neighbor" is only another Jew. So that, either by reading selectively or by finding new meaning to rules we don't like, all Jews don't follow all the rules. The hard part about being Jewish is finding a satisfying way of determining which rules to follow. Ultimately, most Jews do this by joining a specific Jewish community that follows the rules in a certain way, under the leadership of a rabbi with whose interpretation and selection we feel comfortable. Some of the ways people choose a community is whether the rules favored are universalistic or particularistic. Some Jews see Judaism as a religion of ethical, moral, and social rules that tells us how to be better people, drawing closer to all the peoples of the universe. Other Jews see Judaism as a series of rules laid down by God for the Jewish people to survive, grow strong, and protect themselves as a particular, special people. Through talking about these approaches with family members, we clarify why we are Jewish and what rules are important to us.

Howard Adelman
Associate Professor of Jewish Studies
Smith College
Northampton, Massachusetts

If You Are Jewish Do You Have to Follow All the Rules?

From the way the question is formulated, it appears to assume that there is only one religious system or religion that has the name "Jewish." This is not the case: there have been in the course of Jewish history, and there are today, a number of different Jewish religions or Judaisms. Accordingly, the term "Judaism" must always be modified by an adjective that tells us what kind of Jewish religion is being discussed—is it Reform Judaism, Orthodox Judaism, Conservative Judaism, or another kind of Judaism?

I will answer this question from the Reform point of view; that is, I am taking the question to be: "If you are a Reform Jew, do you have to follow all the rules?"

The answer is that Reform Judaism is a polydoxy, a religion of freedom in which every person possesses a fundamental right to ultimate self-authority, or autonomy. Each of us has the right to determine for her/himself what s/he will believe theologically and what observances s/he will keep. Since every Reform Jew possesses freedom, no Reform Jew may perform acts that violate other persons' freedom. Accordingly, we have just one rule that all Reform Jews must follow, and which can be summarized as the "Freedom Covenant." The Freedom Covenant states: every Reform Jew pledges to affirm the ultimate right of all other members of the Reform Jewish community to ultimate self-authority in return for their pledges to affirm her/his own self-authority.

Let us clarify the nature of the Freedom Covenant by taking as examples the freedom a Reform Jew possesses with respect to the liturgy and the meaning of the word "God." A Reformer has the right to use whatever services s/he wishes, and if no satisfactory services exist, the right to

The term "Judaism" must always be modified by an adjective that tells us what kind of Jewish religion is being discussed—is it Reform Judaism, Orthodox Judaism, Conservative Judaism, or another kind of Judaism?

191

make up her/his own or use none at all. Similarly, regarding the term "God," a Reformer has the right to understand the word "God" in whichever way s/he believes true, and if s/he cannot find a meaning for the word "God," s/he has a right to suspend use of the term until s/he has become clear in her/his mind regarding what s/he really believes. Hence, Reform Judaism as a polydoxy is a religion that affirms a person's right to search for truth and authenticity, and to suspend judgment on beliefs and observances so long as the search has not come to an end.

The confusion over rules on the part of Jews comes about because they fail to recognize there is more than one Judaism. Thus it is that Reform Judaism has one rule, observance of the Freedom Covenant, while there are other Judaisms with many rules that their adherents must follow. Orthodox Judaism, for example, has many rules that its followers must observe, and Conservative Judaism also lays down numerous rules. So long as a person achieves clarity regarding which Judaism s/he believes, the rule question will pose no difficulty.

Alvin J. Reines, Professor of Jewish Philosophy
Hebrew Union College-Jewish Institute of Religion
Cincinnati, Ohio

If You Are Jewish Do You Have to Follow All the Rules?

If you are an Orthodox Jew, I believe the answer to this question is, "Yes, you must follow all the rules in the Torah." This is because Orthodox Jews believe that the Torah, both written and oral (Talmud, law codes, etc.), was given at Sinai directly by God to Moses. If this is the case, if the Torah is truly word for word from God, then it is perfect, cannot be challenged, and its laws must be followed exactly as written. There simply is no choice.

On the other hand, as a Liberal Jew I subscribe to the notion that the Torah and other holy texts were written by human beings. As I have studied the texts of our people over the years I have come to the belief that these writers were far closer to God than anyone I know and had keen insight into the way God expects us to live. Their words have stood the test of time and have changed the course of history. It must be remembered, however, that these writers were only human beings, not God. Therefore, what they wrote was not perfect, not infallible, not the final truth.

Therefore, because the texts of our tradition, our rule books, are human documents, if you are a Liberal Jew, no one will tell you that you *must* follow all the rules from our tradition. Yet, even though the rules included in Torah are of human origin, they have stood the test of time and are clearly the products of God-inspired individuals. They must, therefore, be taken very seriously.

In order to take these rules, or *mitzvot* seriously, a person must study them thoroughly, including an understanding of relevant commentaries and historical writings. Once understanding is adequate, I also feel that the individual must experiment with keeping the particular mitzvah. Only after knowledge and experience have been gained is one capable

> In order to take these rules, or *mitzvot* seriously, a person must study them thoroughly, including an understanding of relevant commentaries and historical writings.

193

of making an informed choice about whether or not to follow the rule.

So, as must be clear by now, the Liberal Jew can choose not to follow all of the rules, but it is my feeling that this difficult choice must be made only after a great deal of process and consideration. While it may be easier to simply follow the rule or reject it out of hand, the rewards of this search are great, and that is why I find it exciting to be a Liberal Jew.

Robert E. Tornberg, Educator
Holy Blossom Temple
Toronto, Canada

Why Do We Do Jewish Rituals?

Jewish rituals can add meaning to life in three different ways. First, rituals add rhythm to life. They punctuate the weeks and months of each year, and signal significant times in our lives. They give us the opportunity to differentiate special moments so that they stand out from our ordinary routines. Without rituals, the days and weeks of our lives would merge into one another in a seamless web that would soon become tedious. Rituals give us a way to celebrate the close of a week, the passing of the seasons, and the progress of our lives.

Jewish rituals add a special touch to these special moments. The beautiful prayers, songs, and symbols associated with many rituals add an aesthetic dimension to the moments we celebrate. As rituals are repeated over and over again, they become familiar and comforting, and take on added dimensions. As we grow older, the Passover Seder reminds us not only of the history of our people, but also of our own personal histories, as we recall Passover Seders gone by. The rituals of mourning can be comforting because they prescribe patterns for us to follow at times when our grief can leave us floundering without direction. The Havdalah ceremony, which marks the close of the Sabbath, has a magic all its own, with the flickering of a braided candle lighting up the room, the smell of sweet spices delighting our senses, and the company of family or friends surrounding us with warmth.

Jewish rituals also serve to remind us of the values, hopes and aspirations that are important to us as Jews. The Havdalah ceremony reminds us of the ultimate optimism of Judaism, that one day, indeed, the Messianic Age will arrive. The Passover Seder recounts the story of our people's

Rituals give us a way to celebrate the close of a week, the passing of the seasons, and the progress of our lives.

195

historic liberation, and also calls on us to work toward freedom for all peoples. Many prayers associated with rituals are reminders of the core value of Judaism: that we are partners with God in building a better world. Doing Jewish rituals can remind us to live according to this principle.

Michael Zeldin, Professor of Jewish Education
Hebrew Union College-Jewish Institute of Religion
Los Angeles, California

Why Do We Do Jewish Rituals?

What is a ritual? The way the word is commonly used, it often refers to something that a person does as a task, to a burden that one must do, or else.

It is unfortunate that this same word is used to describe Jewish fulfillment. For example, is praying every morning a ritual, or is it a lovely way of saying thank you to God for being alive and well for another day of meaningful activity?

Is the observance of the Shabbat with all its intricate details a chore and a task, a ritual? Or is it a beautiful way of getting in touch with oneself and one's loved ones, in an atmosphere free from any material creativity, and which allows one to escape from the overwhelming burdens of daily life which obscure what life is about?

Shabbat is a perfect example of a ritual which can be either understood or misconstrued. There are lots of restrictions on Shabbat, but without those restrictions, the fulfillment of Shabbat would be impossible. You cannot have the bliss of a day that is free from outside interference, allowing you to affirm life to the fullest, without the restrictions. You cannot mow the lawn and at the same time be attentive to your spiritual needs. What is seemingly a ritual is, in fact, a discipline which is intended to free the individual from those impediments which interfere with true fulfillment.

And doing it on a regular basis, rather than when you want, assures that it will always be done.

Ritual is a discipline which not only creates governing principles; it also tells us when these have to be done. It is a good education in appreciating that when it comes to life's

We keep to the rituals because the rituals maintain us and keep us on the right path.

important matters, we do not allow things to go by our own whim, but by a higher code. We keep to the rituals because the rituals maintain us and keep us on the right path.

Reuben P. Bulka, Rabbi
Congregation Machzikei Hadas
Ottawa, Canada

Why Do We Do Jewish Rituals?

All peoples and all individuals engage in ritual behavior. In the United States we speak of the ritual of electing a president every four years. Many people do physical exercise as their morning ritual. Rituals can be acts filled with meaning or empty patterns of habitual behavior. In either case, the acts we perform define who we are in the world for ourselves and for other people.

When we speak of doing Jewish rituals, we generally have in mind the performance of religious acts, especially ceremonial acts. Most Jews think of celebrating the Sabbath or having a Seder at Passover as the most common rituals they perform. Over the centuries Jews have developed many reasons for performing Jewish rituals. The writers of the Hebrew Bible believed that God had given the Torah to Moses and the twelve tribes of Israel. Subsequent Jewish tradition understood this to mean that God had revealed all the laws, including the ritual laws, to Moses at Mount Sinai. Doing Jewish rituals meant fulfilling God's commandments (mitzvot).

By the Middle Ages, Jewish thinkers developed a type of literature known as *ta'ame hamitzvot*, "reasons for the commandments." In this literature various reasons were given to help Jews understand why they should observe the commandments. Nevertheless, the basic reason for observance remained the requirement to fulfill God's will. In the modern period many Orthodox Jews still retain this belief. However, most modern Jews who perform Jewish rituals do so for other reasons. Some believe rituals will help preserve the Jewish people. Others think that rituals help deepen a sense of Jewish identity. Still others argue that rituals encourage a community or an individual to develop a

Jewish rituals transmit values, mark special moments in the yearly cycle or the life cycle, and connect people with a sense of God, Jewish experience and each other.

significant religious feeling and closeness to God. Some Jews, of course, do various rituals simply because they are part of the family pattern, and do not seek deeper meanings for their actions.

Whether one believes that God commanded Jews to perform specific rituals or that the performance of rituals is of benefit to the community and the individual, no one doubts that Jewish rituals can have a powerful meaning in people's lives. Ritual acts do not exist in a vacuum. They are part of the life of a community and an individual. Jewish rituals transmit values, mark special moments in the yearly cycle or the life cycle, and connect people with a sense of God, Jewish experience and each other.

Lewis Barth, Professor of Midrash
Hebrew Union College-Jewish Institute of Religion
Los Angeles, California

Is It Important to Wear a Yarmulke and Tallit at Services?

Dressing for prayer is part of our preparation. It helps create the right mood and atmosphere. The tallit has its origin in the biblical verse that tells us to place fringes on the corner of our garments, so that when we look at them, they will remind us of God's commandments (Numbers 15:37-41). The wearing of a tallit is a mitzvah and therefore, when we wrap ourselves in a tallit, we recite the blessing: *Baruch ata Adonai eloheinu melech haolam asher kideshanu bemitzvotav vetsivanu lehitatef batsitsit,* "We praise You Adonai our God, Ruler of the universe, who sanctifies us with commandments and commands us to wrap ourselves in a fringed garment."

A midrashic text pictures God as arising each morning and putting on a tallit of light. So, in putting on a tallit, we imitate God. The imitation of God is an important theological concept in Judaism. We are taught that just as God visits the sick, clothes the naked, and feeds the hungry, so should we. Being holy means imitating God. By symbolically praying the way God prays, we focus on the activity of prayer and its importance. Further, it helps develop the proper frame of mind to make our prayer experience significant. When I put on a tallit I feel enwrapped by God's presence and feel responsible for observing the *mitzvot*.

The yarmulke, like the tallit, is an authentic garment of Jewish prayer. By putting it on we identify with being Jewish and we put ourselves into a prayerful mood. In the Middle East, where Judaism was born, covering one's head is a sign of respect. Therefore, when we enter the synagogue to pray, our wearing a yarmulke is one sign of respect for God. It is a concrete way of saying that we recognize that we are standing in God's presence. The yarmulke can be an effective way of saying that the activity we are about to

> The yarmulke, like the tallit, is an authentic garment of Jewish prayer. By putting it on we identify with being Jewish and we put ourselves into a prayer mood.

201

engage in is important. Just as a baseball player goes on the field wearing a team cap, so we put on the yarmulke to say that we want to be part of God's team.

In Reform Judaism our attitude toward the wearing of yarmulke and tallit has undergone a significant change. When I grew up in the Reform movement, they were prohibited. Now, in most congregations, they have become an option and in some places they are now the norm. While the wearing of tallit or yarmulke should not be made mandatory, wearing one or both at services can be very important. They are both authentic garments of Jewish worship and symbols of Jewish identity. By wearing them at services we make worship a unique time. It is like putting on a uniform to show that we all belong to the same team and are ready to play.

The use of special modes of dress can make us more conscious of our Jewishness and the importance of the mitzvah of prayer. While the yarmulke and tallit can be a very significant means of enhancing worship for some, the wearing of these garments does not make us better than those who choose not to wear them.

Peter S. Knobel, Rabbi
Beth Emet-The Free Synagogue
Evanston, Illinois

Is It Important to Wear a Yarmulke and Tallit at Services?

Let me respond in a roundabout way. I was raised in a home where classical Reform Judaism was practiced. My family members were proud Jews, temple-going Jews. My grandfather was president of a major Reform congregation, and my grandmother blessed each child and grandchild every Erev Shabbat. Her blessing was a highlight of my week. But as Reform Jews fifty years ago, a yarmulke and tallit were not part of our Judaism. To us, only Orthodox and Conservative Jews wore them. Our *not* wearing them was to us a symbol of pride, identity, and Reform uniqueness.

For me, I like the idea of having a special time, in temple, accompanied by special Jewish symbols. It unites me with my fellow Jews. And so, I wear my Jewish uniform of choice.

But time, growth, Hitler, the Holocaust, the State of Israel, all had their effect on me. The changes came gradually, almost imperceptibly. Gradually I came to realize that we Jews were one people, and that differences in the *way* we did things were not so important any more. I sensed the need to be more part of my people than apart from them.

A change in my attitude toward Jewish ritual and identity symbols accompanied the other changes. I started to give the specifics of Judaism a chance. I rejected some and embraced others. But I came to understand and respect even those I chose not to follow. Today, I would not (and will not) be told that I must do this or *cannot* do that. Forcing one's religious life is not Reform Judaism. But I am open now in a way I was not fifty years ago. And as a Reform Jew, I choose on the basis of my knowledge, my commitment, and my own best thinking.

As for the yarmulke and tallit, I know that the origins of the tallit are biblical, but that the origins of the yarmulke are much later, and clouded in uncertainty about its universal usage. I find those facts interesting but not important.

What has become important to me is that when I go to temple, I now *prefer* to wear a yarmulke and tallit. I don't do it because Halacha (Jewish law) commands me. I simply call it "my Jewish uniform of choice." I can worship without them also; they are not idols. But I feel a bit more Jewish when I wear them, and that makes me feel good.

Are they necessary? No!

Are they desirable: It depends on how each individual feels about these matters. I think yes.

For me, I like the idea of having a special time, in temple, accompanied by special Jewish symbols. It unites me with my fellow Jews. And so, I wear my Jewish uniform of choice.

Frank Sundheim, Director
Southeast Council
Union of American Hebrew Congregations
Miami, Florida

What Is So Important About Bar/Bat Mitzvah?

Among my most cherished possessions is a violin that belonged to my grandfather. I learned to play it as a child (though I couldn't wait to finish my weekly lesson and run out to play ball with my friends). These days, I often take the instrument out of its case to feel the wood and to hold it in my hands. It is a precious link between my grandfather and me—a symbol of our family's musical tradition.

I also have my grandfather's tefillin. As a teenager I learned how to put them on. I tried praying with them a few times—but now they rest in a soft bag in my dresser drawer. The leather is old and cracked. Still, my grandfather's tefillin are another precious connection—a symbol of our family's Jewish tradition.

What do a violin and tefillin have to do with each other and with the Bar/Bat Mitzvah experience? When things have deep meaning for us, we want to pass them on to our children and grandchildren. These are our traditions. They can either sit in a closet and be forgotten or be used to bring enjoyment and meaning to our lives. But here's the catch: to play an instrument or pray with tefillin you have to know how—like most everything in life, they require learning a skill.

"Doing Jewishly" requires learning some basic skills. The years leading up to Bar/Bat Mitzvah are a fine time for learning the skills, the nitty-gritty of being Jewish. Why now and not later? Reading Torah, chanting blessings and prayers, learning rituals, and practicing Jewish values cannot be accomplished overnight. It takes years of practice to do these things comfortably. Yes, it's hard, I tell my students, but if it wasn't hard you wouldn't be as proud of your accomplishments.

Becoming a Bar or Bat Mitzvah is more than reading a Haftarah or chanting a blessing. It means looking at who we are through a Jewish lens. It means engaging in a relationship with the tradition—asking questions, seeking answers, finding meaning.

205

Becoming a Bar or Bat Mitzvah is more than reading a Haftarah or chanting a blessing. It means looking at who we are through a Jewish lens. It means engaging in a relationship with the tradition—asking questions, seeking answers, finding meaning. It starts with parents and teachers who are themselves in love with Jewish tradition. The foundation for a lifetime of Jewish learning begins with simple things: candles and Kiddush, challah, latkes, and lulavs—the tastes and smells and sensory experiences available to all, but especially memorable for children. It continues with good books, patient teachers, summers at a Jewish camp, and lots and lots of practice. The example we set for our children will be the one they follow.

One of the most important answers to the question above is that those children who have a positive Bar/Bat Mitzvah experience will want to replicate the experience for *their* children. And that is what tradition is all about.

Jeff Klepper, Cantor
Beth Emet-The Free Synagogue
Evanston, Illinois

What Is So Important About Bar/Bat Mitzvah?

"And you will teach it diligently to your children" (Deuteronomy 11:19). Judaic and Hebrew study is really a lifetime endeavor. Bar/Bat Mitzvah can never be thought of as an isolated event, but rather as one of the highlights in one's Jewish life. Preparation for Bar/Bat Mitzvah, therefore, has as much to do with what has been learned at home, at Hebrew school and at Religious School as it does with what has been learned during the weeks and months immediately prior to the Bar/Bat Mitzvah.

Bar/Bat Mitzvah is a very important rite of passage in our Jewish children's lives. Because no one can possibly be spiritually mature at the age of thirteen, we can never expect that Bar/Bat Mitzvah represents the end of one's religious education. But it represents for each child an opportunity to demonstrate to *Kehillat Yisrael*—the Jewish community—what has been learned during his/her Judaic and Hebrew studies: to lead a congregation in prayer and worship, to read from Torah and Haftarah, to publicly share personal thoughts about the entire experience.

Many people participate in the process of preparing for Bar/Bat Mitzvah. The rabbi, the cantor, the Hebrew school, the religious school, and of course, the student and his/her family—each has an important role to play in this process. And the caring, dedicated participation of every person will ensure the most powerful, memorable event in each Bar/Bat Mitzvah's life.

Bar/Bat Mitzvah is really a family event. From the day the date is set, the household begins humming with the excitement of preparations. While the ultimate responsibility to study and learn rests on the student, the parent's role in the whole process can impact greatly on the student's feelings about this event.

For the young Jew, Bar/Bat Mitzvah represents a powerful lesson in continuity. As each Bar/Bat Mitzvah student takes the Torah into his/her heart, he/she touches every Jew who came before and every Jew who will come after, for generations.

For the young Jew, Bar/Bat Mitzvah represents a powerful lesson in continuity. As each Bar/Bat Mitzvah student takes the Torah into his/her heart, he/she touches every Jew who came before and every Jew who will come after, for generations. As each Bar/Bat Mitzvah reads the Torah portion and the Haftarah designated for that special day, he/she touches every Jew in every city of the world who is reading that very same Torah portion and Haftarah, and every Jew who read it as part of the annual cycle for thousands of years past, and every Jew who *will* read it each year, well into the future.

Vicki L. Axe, Cantor
Temple Israel
Columbus, Ohio

Why Don't Jewish People Celebrate Christmas?

Holidays are important celebrations. They teach us about our history; they remind us of the customs and traditions of our family and our people. Religious holidays help us learn about our religious faith and beliefs; they celebrate the historic events and spiritual lessons of our religion.

Jewish people celebrate Jewish holidays. And Christians celebrate Christian holidays. We Jews observe our own holidays because they help us to learn about Judaism and to follow Jewish traditions and rituals. Jewish people don't celebrate Christmas because it is not a Jewish holiday. Christmas is a Christian holiday.

It is not appropriate for Jews to celebrate Christmas. When Jews celebrate it, it is insulting our Christian friends and neighbors. Jews may see Christmas as a fun holiday, filled with fancy trees, many gifts, lots of public decorations and glitter. It is dazzling, exciting, and attractive during the winter season. But to a Christian, Christmas has a much deeper meaning. Christmas is one of the holiest and most special days of the year. It is a religious event, which commemorates the birth of Jesus, the Lord and Savior of Christianity. When Jews, who do not believe in the Christian faith, try to observe the holiday, they are belittling Christianity and its faith.

Judaism has its own holidays. And Jews celebrate them throughout the year. Each week, we honor the Sabbath with candles and challah and shiny Kiddush cups. In the fall, we build booths outside for Sukkot, complete with fruits and decorations. The Sabbath and Sukkot teach us important lessons about Judaism and about our Jewish history.

In the winter, Jews observe Hanukah. This is the special week-long festival that teaches us about an important time in our Jewish history. Hanukah tells the story of a small

Jewish people don't celebrate Christmas because it is not our holiday. Jewish people celebrate Hanukah and other Jewish holidays.

209

group of Jewish people who waged a battle against their enemies. These enemies wanted to force the Jews to celebrate non-Jewish customs and festivals. Jews fought, nearly two thousand years ago, so that they and all Jews could live freely and could observe the holidays of our faith. Jews today can be grateful that we have our own holidays and can observe them as we choose.

Jewish people don't celebrate Christmas because it is not our holiday. Jewish people celebrate Hanukah and other Jewish holidays.

Beth H. Klafter, Educational Director
Temple Judea
Manhasset, New York

Why Don't Jewish People Celebrate Christmas?

"I am Hanukah, and Tiffany is Christmas," Alexandra told her mother one day after a serious discussion in the kindergarten yard. These two girls, playing jump rope, were trying to find out each other's religion but could not remember the words.

In order to answer the question "Why don't Jews celebrate Christmas?" we need to look at the issue of religious identity in a broader context. How do children form a sense of religious identity? What do we mean when we use the term "celebrate"? How can families that have non-Jewish members be together during December in a way that expresses love for all relatives?

Parents who choose to create a Jewish identity for their children might draw an analogy between the discussion of Christmas and a familiar parenting principle. Let us imagine a toddler who is approaching a coffee table. On the table we find a piece of crystal. Every adult in the room knows that the toddler is about to pick up the crystal and bang it on the table. Before that can happen a parent will move into action, take the crystal away, and give the toddler a soft stuffed animal to bang on the table. No wise parent would just take away the shiny object without replacing it with a soft one.

The toddler learns, "I can look at the shiny object, it is very special to the people who own it, but it is not mine. I cannot bang it on the table."

He or she also learns, "The soft object is mine." It may be that familiar, warm, soft old friend that makes the toddler feel safe in the world. As children grow older, they do not need to take the physical object with them. If they were given the object at critical moments, it may become a source of security and strength.

Often, the dialogue regarding Christmas in a Jewish home is focused on the process of taking away the shiny object—Christmas. I recommend that the focus *should* rather be on the process of handing the child the soft cuddly animal—creating a sense of Jewish identity.

How can parents who choose to create a Jewish identity give children a sense of positive religious identity when Christmas can seem so pervasive and appealing in December?

Children develop a sense of religious identity both by what they are told and, even more, by what they do in their homes. The Jewish calendar is rich with opportunities for families to create a warm positive Jewish identity. Holidays occur frequently, and Shabbat weekly throughout the year.

It is quite possible for Jews with a clear sense of their own religious identity to participate as guests at a Christmas event of a friend or family member. Parents should keep in mind the distinction between celebrating a holiday as our own and being with family members or friends to help them celebrate a holiday which is theirs. Being a guest at a religious celebration is an idea that goes in both directions. What about the thought of reciprocating an invitation to a Christmas party with an invitation to a Shabbat dinner?

Now we return to Tiffany and Alexandra. They may not have remembered the words "Jewish" and "Christian," but they did have a clear, comfortable understanding that Jews celebrate Hanukah and Christians celebrate Christmas. We hope the adults in their world have the loving appreciation of the clear vision of Tiffany and Alexandra.

Arlene Sarah Chernow, Outreach Coordinator
Pacific Southwest Council
Union of American Hebrew Congregations
Los Angeles, California

ABOUT THE EDITORS

David P. Kasakove is Director of Media and Communications in the Department for Religious Education at the Union of American Hebrew Congregations. He is the executive editor of *Compass Magazine: New Directions for Jewish Education*, Director of the UAHC TV & Film Institute, and textbook editor for the UAHC Press. David holds a Master's Degree in religious education from Hebrew Union College-Jewish Institute of Religion, New York. He is the co-author of *Hebrew, Holidays and Heroes: A Jewish Fun Book.*

Rabbi Kerry M. Olitzky, D.H.L., is Director of the School of Education at Hebrew Union College-Jewish Institute of Religion in New York. He is at the forefront of innovative Jewish education. He is the author of numerous books, monographs, and articles, including *The How To Handbook for Jewish Living* and *Twelve Jewish Steps to Recovery: A Personal Guide to Turning Away from Alcoholism and Other Addictions.* Dr. Olitzky is executive curriculum coordinator for *Shofar* magazine and producer/moderator of "Message of Israel," broadcast on the ABC Radio Network.

Rabbi Steven M. Rosman, Ph.D., is rabbi of Jewish Family Congregation, South Salem, New York. He is a master storyteller and author of *Sidrah Stories: A Torah Companion*; *Deena the Dameselfly*; and co-author of *Eight Tales for Eight Nights.* He has lectured internationally on the uses of story and imagery in education, healing, and spiritual growth. In 1990 he was Governor Mario Cuomo's featured storyteller at the New York governor's annual winter holiday event.

INDEX